God's Love for Me

An Ezra 710 Plan Bible Study

This Bible study on **God's Love for Me** is part of the Ezra 7^{10} ™ series of publications. It is also part of a larger three-book discipleship program called the *Ezra 7^{10} Plan*. Specifically **God's Love for Me** is a *Discovery Bible study* included as part of Book 1 - ***First Love:*** *A Heart to Understand.* For more information about this discipleship series please go to the program web site at http://www.ezra710plan.org

God's Love for Me

Geoseff Doulos

An Ezra 710 Plan Bible Study

Cover Graphic: Heart_sweetheartValentine –by Jouni Paavilainen: www.ChristianPhotos.Net

Editor-in-Chief: Judy Kissinger

God's Love for Me

Front Royal, VA 22630

Ezra 710 publications
ISBN–13: 978-0-6154-451-13
ISBN–10: 0-6154-451-1x

To the Glory of God

TABLE OF CONTENTS

God's Love for Me

Discovery

God's Love for Me

Why this study

In the following pages we will be diving into a detailed study of selected verses of the *love* chapter (thirteen) of the Book of First Corinthians. While plenty of research will be provided, this will be our chance to do some Biblical digging, critical thinking, and summarizing of our thoughts about God's love for us.

There is the impression in some circles that the Lord was a God of judgment in the Old Testament but a God of love in the New Testament. A great study would actually be on judgment in the Old Testament. If we properly discern who receives judgment and why, and how the Lord spares the rest, we will discover that judgment is simply another characteristic of love. And of course, if we hone in on Jesus' life, we will see the same *Old Testament* judgment displayed in the New Testament. This comes as no surprise since the Lord never changes and His love never fails.

We can approach this study with excitement because of that fact. We are not studying about a God who is arbitrary and capricious about how He deals with His creation. Many misconceptions about the Lord exist because people do not read the Bible regularly. They remember bits and pieces while never actually having read the Bible through from cover to cover on a continual basis. One phrase that Jesus mentions more than once in the New Testament when dealing with doubters is, *have you not read...*

If we had a thousand-piece puzzle and put it together using only 250 pieces, we would not have a good idea of the true picture in front of us. We could speculate all we want, but until we have all the pieces placed in their proper context our opinions most likely would be in error.

The fact is that the Old Testament contains so many instances of God's love that to conclude otherwise would simply be wrong, to put it bluntly. That is why for the Bible study that follows, many of the examples of God's love have been taken from the Old Testament. It is our hope that this study will serve a two-fold purpose. For those of us new to faith in the Lord Jesus Christ, it will be our chance to be awestruck at the height, depth and breadth of the love God has for us. It is truly breathtaking. For those who have been believers for a while (maybe a long while), this is our chance to remember and embrace again the fullness of God's love for us. When we discover how much God loves us, we will begin to love others in the same way. God's love for us becomes a platform from which we feel safe and secure enough to open our hearts to love others.

For young and old, this will firmly establish and strengthen our spiritual foundation. We will begin to build up our spiritual temple as we see God as never before. We will continue to make more and more room for His Spirit to fill us and strengthen us to serve.

What the study covers

The Bible study covers the following aspects of love in detail:

Is patient	*Is kind*	*Is not jealous*	*Does not brag*	*Is not arrogant*
Does not act unbecomingly	*Does not seek its own*	*Is not provoked*	*Does not take into account a wrong suffered*	*Does not rejoice in unrighteous-ness*
Rejoices with the truth	*Bears*	*Believes*	*Hopes*	*Endures*
Never fails				

For each of the above characteristics some background material has been provided, including famous quotes and stories as well as a comic strip. We will then look up an Old Testament example of this characteristic. From there, we will record our thoughts on that passage, recall instances of how the Lord has displayed this action in our life, and really think about how specifically we can pattern our life after this Godly characteristic.

We should make sure before we make these applications that we pray first, be as specific as possible, and set a goal that is attainable. These applications can take the form of knowledge (remembering something we learned), attitude (a new way of thinking), and action (either starting or stopping an action as warranted).

Finally we will have some space to prepare a little teaching on what we have just learned so we can easily pass it on to others. Here we can put some thoughts down that will help us remember how to explain this aspect of love to others. We can create an acronym or an illustration and/or memorize a key verse that summarizes the meaning, or memorize a parable or story that brings out the meaning. Of course, sharing from personal experience is always a good teacher. Keep it simple. This exercise of creating teaching points will force us to digest more thoroughly all the material that we have learned. Note that this teaching may be revised over time, and feel free to circle back to this Bible study many times. Our teaching may also make for a good devotion to share with others. There is an extra credit section that follows our teaching points that is designed to stimulate our thinking even more.

Suggested Schedule

Try and finish a Bible study on two characteristics of love each week. This will total eight weeks. Note that there are two more optional (but highly recommended) homework assignments in the final section titled *Encore*. They should be completed during what would be week nine.

Some Final Thoughts Before We Begin the Study

While it is true that the Lord brings people into our lives to encourage us and to display for us in person His many qualities, it is also true that we live in a world that displays every form of ungodliness. This tends to affect us negatively and makes it hard to see God's love shining through. Many people face issues of fear, doubt and low self-esteem, and find it hard to comprehend how much the Lord loves them. Now one answer for this may be to surround ourselves with godly people as much as possible. But this is not possible to achieve every hour of the day.

There is something more we must do: To experience the fullness of God's love, we need first and foremost to draw upon God's love for us directly from the Lord Himself. People fail, and people will let us down, but God will never let us down.

Remember that. The Lord designed His people to function as a body, as a team, but our main source of inspiration individually should always be from the Lord Himself. We need to view correctly how God sees us. We need to combat the lies and deception we are being fed with the truth about the love God has for us. And that is what this study is all about. We will see God as never before. We will, perhaps for the first time in our life, realize how much we are truly treasured by the Lord.

When we fully grasp the depth of love that the King of Kings and Lord of Lords has for us as His children, it is truly humbling, and yet at the same time empowering. Once we see how much we are loved, the fog will lift. We will then clearly see the goal — and what a lofty goal. Jesus sets the bar for us and communicates in no uncertain terms our goal: simply put, perfection. Ouch! Just when we were feeling so comfortable!

The next big step in fully comprehending God's love for us is when we begin to live it out. This step is when we dare to exhibit His love to all people and not just to people who will love us back. This is where many — so many — fail to experience the richness of His love. Remember when Jesus clarified what it meant to *love your neighbor as yourself ?* Remember when He introduced a new commandment *Love others as I have loved you?* This was not really new but it put a simple yet profound perspective on loving others.

His is a selfless love, not desiring anything in return. He is also saying *do what I do.* The great thing about this is that we are not just adhering to rules and regulations, but we are imitating a person who has gone before us and left us many examples to follow. Examples abound in the Old Testament as well. Let us read His view of perfection as stated in Matthew chapter five.

Matthew 5:43-48 *You have heard that it was said, "You shall love your neighbor and hate your enemy." But I say to you, love your enemies and pray for those who persecute you, so that you may be sons of your Father who is in heaven; for He causes His sun to rise on the evil and the good, and sends rain on the righteous and the unrighteous. For if you love those who love you, what reward do you have? Do not even the tax collectors do the same? If you greet only your brothers, what more are you doing than others? Do not even the Gentiles do the same?" Therefore you are to be perfect, as your heavenly Father is perfect.*

Also take a look at First John chapter four (paragraph breaks are author's for emphasis).

1 John 4: 7-21 *Beloved, let us love one another, for love is from God; and everyone who loves is born of God and knows God.*

The one who does not love does not know God, for God is love. By this the love of God was manifested in us that God has sent His only begotten Son into the world so that we might live through Him. In this is love, not that we loved God, but that He loved us and sent His Son to be the propitiation for our sins.

Beloved, if God so loved us, we also ought to love one another. No one has seen God at any time; if we love one another, God abides in us, and His love is perfected in us. By this we know that we abide in Him and He in us, because He has given us of His Spirit. We have seen and testify that the Father has sent the Son to be the Savior of the world. Whoever confesses that Jesus is the Son of God, God abides in him, and he in God. We have come to know and have believed the love which God has for us.

God is love, and the one who abides in love abides in God, and God abides in him. By this, love is perfected with us, so that we may have confidence in the day of judgment; because as He is, so also are we in this world.

There is no fear in love; but perfect love casts out fear, because fear involves punishment, and the one who fears is not perfected in love.

We love, because He first loved us. If someone says, "I love God," and hates his brother, he is a liar; for the one who does not love his brother whom he has seen, cannot love God whom he has not seen.

And this commandment we have from Him, that the one who loves God should love his brother also.

And finally the goal of this study could not be stated any better than in Ephesians chapter three.

Ephesians 3:14-19 *For this reason I bow my knees before the Father, from whom every family in heaven and on earth derives its name, that He would grant you, according to the riches of His glory, to be strengthened with power through His Spirit in the inner man, so that Christ may dwell in your hearts through faith; and that you, being rooted and grounded in love, may be able to comprehend with all the saints what is the breadth and length and height and depth, and to know the love of Christ which surpasses knowledge, that you may be filled up to all the fullness of God.*

It is interesting to note that the apostle Paul is writing this to the church at Ephesus, expressing his hope for them to experience the depths of God's love, and yet dozens of years later another apostle, John, writes to a church in the Book of Revelation admonishing them because they have lost their first love. Guess what church it was.

'Nuff said — now we need to start putting those puzzle pieces together!

Note that many of the quotes in the following sections can be found in an excellent resource, the *Encyclopedia of 7700 illustrations: A treasury of illustrations, anecdotes, facts and quotations for pastors, teachers and Christian workers, by Tan, P. L. (1996, c1979). Garland TX: Bible Communications.*

CHARACTERISTIC OF LOVE

Discussion

Biblical patience includes the idea of long-suffering or being long-tempered (as opposed to being short-tempered). In fact, the Greek word translated as *being patient* (verb) or *patience* (noun) includes the concept *long* within the word itself. The verb in Greek is μακροθυμέω (*makrothumeō).* It is a compound of two words: μακρὸς (*macros*) meaning *long* or *long-lasting*, or for distances, *a long way away*; and θυμόω (*thumoō*) meaning *to become angry, to become incensed with wrath.* So literally translated, exhibiting patience means you take a very long time before you become angry. Instead of having a short fuse, you have a very long fuse. It is identical in the Hebrew, where the Hebrew word for *long* is usually paired with another word such as *anger*, denoting that God is *slow* (or *long*) *to anger.* It is interesting to note that the Greek translation of the Old Testament (*The Septuagint*, usually denoted as *LXX*) most often translates the Hebrew expression *slow to anger* with the Greek *makrothumeō.* Also note that patience is a fruit of the Spirit as detailed in Galatians 5:22.

Biblical patience is something we exercise. In our study verse, the words *is patient* are actually used as a verb in the original Greek. The more literal translation would be *love is being patient.* Perhaps one way to think of how to practice patience would be to think of what makes us angry. Does this mean that practicing patience means never being angry? Good point. So how do we know when it is acceptable to be angry or when patience should be displayed? What is God's view of patience? How does God want us to practice patience?

By looking up verses that contain patience or patient we can get a good idea of God's view of things. We could do an exhaustive study of this topic if we used a thesaurus to look up similar words, such as long-suffering, forgiving, lenient, etc.

Here are just a few to read.

God's Patience Toward Us	
2 Peter 3:9 *The Lord is not slow about His promise, as some count slowness, but is patient toward you, not wishing for any to perish but for all to come to repentance.*	Romans 2:4 *Or do you think lightly of the riches of His kindness and tolerance and patience, not knowing that the kindness of God leads you to repentance?*

God Requests Our Patience	
Psalm 37:7 *Rest in the Lord and wait patiently for Him...*	Hebrews 6:12 *so that you will not be sluggish, but imitators of those who through faith and patience inherit the promises.*

Examples of Our Patience Toward Others	
2 Timothy 4:2 *preach the word; be ready in season and out of season; reprove, rebuke, exhort, with great patience and instruction.*	
1 Thessalonians 5:14 *We urge you, brethren, admonish the unruly, encourage the fainthearted, help the weak, be patient with everyone.*	James 5:10 *As an example, brethren, of suffering and patience, take the prophets who spoke in the name of the Lord.*

By reading the verses above we may reach a few conclusions about patience. To discover God's perspective on patience we must discover His goal for all the qualities of love. It is clear from the verses above that He is patient when He sees into the very heart of people. He can see that there is still room for change, for repentance, for turning their life around towards His way, which is the goal. Even from the cross Jesus saw into the hearts of His accusers and could discern that they really did not know what they were doing, and perhaps there was still hope for them. That is why He asked the Father to forgive them. This is the very reason we need to display patience even toward our *enemies*. (We can, however, safely discount the Hitler and Nero-types out there.) This may be easier when we know the people we see, such as our friends and family. However, we all know that certain people try our patience more than others. Perhaps the Lord has placed these people in our path to help lengthen our *long* in our ability to display long-suffering.

Patience is thus a key ingredient in being able to work well with people. People who have little patience tend also to be those who are insensitive and unreasonable. Patience is needed as we work with co-workers, children, students, and disciples. We need to give people time to learn things and tailor our expectations according to the person. Patience is not easily upset when someone makes a mistake. We should not expect the exact same progress from everyone. God treats us as individuals. We should not be so quick to give up or give out on others. Remember, if we are quick to anger, we may also be slow to realize the potential in others. Conversely if we are slow to anger, we may be quick to see that progress is indeed being made. We should strive for the latter.

Proverbs 19:11 *A man's discretion makes him slow to anger, And it is his glory to overlook a transgression.*

The Lord exhibits anger when people resolutely decide to go their own way. In these situations, warnings, admonitions, and even rebukes may be warranted to open people's eyes to their sinful ways. That is tough love. We need to exhibit patience even when we admonish others. We should not fly off the handle or say something we will regret. Thus we exhibit patience in dealing with slow learners and those who are clearly going down the wrong path. Now remember how long it may have taken us to repent and place our faith in the Lord. The Lord had to wait for us patiently all that time. Recall Moses' first encounter with the Lord at the burning bush. Despite Moses' own reservations about his shortcomings, God saw into his heart and knew he was the man for the job. The Lord started to become angry when it appeared that Moses was going to resolutely turn down the offer, but Moses was so assured by God's continual encouragement and exhortation that he accepted the task. His worries about his own inabilities were overcome by God's assurance that his own weaknesses would be replaced with God's strengths. We need to keep this in mind when we interact with others, especially those of us who are parents, ministry leaders, teachers, coaches, etc. We should keep Moses in mind when we are waiting for the promises of God. We can be patient because we know that the Lord desires His best for us.

Our patience and sensitivity toward others and our patience in following the Lord will help us remove any barriers that may prevent us from having good relationships. Perhaps that is why patience is mentioned first in this list and why it is a key fruit of the Spirit.

Finally, let us view patience as it is needed for different relational groups. Some of the people we interact with on a daily basis may be placed into three very broad categories, each with its own challenges. One group includes all the people who are in an authoritative position over us. This would include the Lord Himself, but also includes church leaders; employers; federal, state and local government, etc. Another group includes those that we exhibit authority over, such as children, employees, various groups in the church, etc. The third group represents those personal challenges. These are people we have a hard time dealing with for a variety of reasons. Each group tries our patience in different ways. Those in authority may challenge our pride, as we may disagree with the way they do things. Those we lead and/or teach may challenge our authority or become discipline problems. Or perhaps we think they are not progressing as fast as we think they should. Those hard-to-get-along-with people perhaps challenge us the most to love whom we think may be unlovable. Think about these situations. Does anyone come to mind? Perhaps the Lord is reminding us to be patient with certain people in the same way as the Lord has been patient with us.

We will all go through experiences in which we find it hard to practice patience, perhaps even being patient with the Lord Himself. It is these times in which our patience has room for growth. We should not say that we will never be able to be patient with or work with someone. The Lord will help us increase our capacity for patience and sensitivity. It may take some time, but do not lock the door on patience. Sadly, once we decide that we will limit our patience or who we want to associate or deal with, our spiritual life in general will begin to suffer. We can just hear the Lord saying: *It's great that you love folks who love you back or you get along with easily. Now what about those who you do not even want to be around? What about those who you think won't amount to anything? I want you to work with them and be patient with them too. I do not want you to just be in a holy huddle, or stay in click groups all your life.*

One day we might wake up and feel that we have more enemies than friends. If we are patient with them while we seek guidance from the Lord, our entire perspective may change.

Perhaps these final words will also inspire us to gain more patience!

Quotes

John and Charles Wesley were blessed with a patient mother. At one time her husband said, "I marvel at your patience! You have told that child the same thing twenty times!" Susanna Wesley looked fondly at the child. She said, "Had I spoken the matter only nineteen times, I should have lost all my labor."
— Choice Gleanings

A man is a hero, not because he is braver than anyone else, but because he is brave for ten minutes longer. — Emerson

Two Christians were driving through an area where the road was being widened. At the end of the repair zone, a sign informed travelers, "Construction Ended. Thank You for Your Patience." "I think that would make an appropriate epitaph for my life," said one of the Christians.

XOgesis

KJ: "My mom says I have a short tempter. Does that mean I can't reach others to tempt them?"

Naz: "Knowing you it probably means you have no patience. Your mom no doubt said you have a short temper."

KJ: "Hey are you calling me names, why I oughta..."

Naz: "See what I mean, you get angry easily, you have a short temper."

KJ: "I can't help it. I'm short. Maybe when I grow taller I'll have a longer temper?!"

Naz: "Let's hope so. In the meantime, I guess we'll have to be patient with you, Shorty!"

OLD TESTAMENT EXAMPLES [Gen 18:16-33] [Book of Jonah]

Describe how the LORD displays ***Patience*** in these passages.

Describe how the LORD has been ***Patient*** with you and/or someone that you know.

List a way you will be ***Patient*** this week. Prepare a concise teaching on ***Patience***.

My Application:

My Lesson Plan

Extra Credit – Pick any of the 10 commandments and think about how being ***Patient*** will help you fulfill the commandment.

CHARACTERISTIC OF LOVE

Discussion

Biblical kindness includes the idea that we are bringing some benefit to another person. When we have been treated with kindness, our life has benefited in some way, big or small. In fact, *Merriam-Webster's* dictionary defines benefit as *an act of kindness*. The word *benefit* from the Latin (*bene factum*) literally means *to do good*.

The word for *to be kind* or *kindness* in the Hebrew has a very interesting etymology. The verb *to be kind* in the Hebrew is חָסַד, (chasad) and the verb, *to be reproached* or *ashamed* share the exact same spelling. The same holds true for the noun forms (i.e., kindness and shame). They both come from a root word that means *eager zeal* or *desire* according to *The Enhanced Brown-Driver-Briggs Hebrew and English Lexicon*. So if our zeal is for good it leads to acts of kindness and if our zeal is morally destitute it leads to shame and reproach. Also, in the Greek, the words *is kind* in 1 Corinthians 13:4, are actually used as a verb, and so should be translated as *love is being kind* or *love is showing acts of kindness*.

The reason this etymology is discussed is to highlight the fact that being kind is accompanied by zeal and enthusiasm. It is not meant to be for the exclusive domain of the quiet and elderly. When we are being kind our purpose is to improve the lives of those around us by providing them some tangible benefit. When we are described as being a kind person, our life in part serves to benefit others. It goes without saying that a kind person is a selfless person. It is hard to be self-absorbed and yet still plan our daily activities so that we will be a blessing to others. How can we remove our self from our burdens so that we will be able to remove burdens from others? That is a good question. It is answered in kindness.

It is answered in a simple question we can ask ourselves every day. How can I benefit another person today?

Developing kindness is a process, and the following will help us start. First, meditate on the following verse from Philippians:

Philippians 2:3-4 *Do nothing from selfishness or empty conceit, but with humility of mind regard one another as more important than yourselves; do not merely look out for your own personal interests, but also for the interests of others.*

To be truly kind we need to put our own personal interests in their proper priority. The Lord always comes first; that is a given. What happens after that often becomes fuzzy. Although we go to the Lord for our help and sustenance, it is not meant to be a closed loop. While we are being helped we need to be on the lookout to help others. This is easy to do with some and much harder with others. Do we think the Lord puts people in our paths to *stretch* our capacity for kindness? Absolutely. Note that *kindness*, like *patience* we just studied, is a fruit of the Spirit as detailed in Galatians 5:22.

We should not say we will never be kind to someone who is unkind to us, for the Lord experiences this every day. We should aspire to be like Christ. If He sends blessings and healings on the unjust and unloving, so should we. Consider the many people Jesus healed and yet did not show Him any appreciation. What motivated Jesus to help them? It was kindness. It was His way of showing us, do as I do, even to ungrateful people.

Kindness demands no thanks but seeks its reward in the blessing it bestows on its recipients. Kindness is no doormat but rather a willing enthusiastic servant. Kindness is Joseph who made himself blind to his surroundings and benefited his fellow prisoners. Kindness is Ruth who left all to be a blessing to her mother-in-law. When we seek only our own interests our life is like a closed pool of water that becomes more stagnant as each year passes. We can become stingy and unsympathetic, completely oblivious to the opportunities we have to benefit others.

When we seek to live also for the benefit of others, the dam will break and refreshing waters of life will continually pour forth from our soul, enriching the lives of many and ours as well.

John 7:38 *He who believes in Me, as the Scripture said, 'From his innermost being will flow rivers of living water.'*

Consider the following verses as well.

God's Kindness Toward Us	
Psalm 106:7 *Our fathers in Egypt did not understand Your wonders; They did not remember Your abundant kindnesses,*	Psalm 145:17 *The Lord is righteous in all His ways And kind in all His deeds.*
Luke 6:35 *But love your enemies, and do good, and lend, expecting nothing in return; and your reward will be great, and you will be sons of the Most High; for He Himself is kind to ungrateful and evil men.*	

God Requests Our Kindness	
Galatians 5:22 *But the fruit of the Spirit is love, joy, peace, patience, kindness, goodness, faithfulness,*	Colossians 3:12 *So, as those who have been chosen of God, holy and beloved, put on a heart of compassion, kindness, humility, gentleness and patience;*
Ephesians 4:32 *Be kind to one another, tender-hearted, forgiving each other, just as God in Christ also has forgiven you.*	Micah 6:8 *He has told you, O man, what is good; And what does the Lord require of you But to do justice, to love kindness, And to walk humbly with your God?*

Examples of Our Kindness Toward Others	
2 Samuel 9:1 *Then David said, "Is there yet anyone left of the house of Saul, that I may show him kindness for Jonathan's sake?*	Proverbs 31:26 *She opens her mouth in wisdom, And the teaching of kindness is on her tongue.*
2 Timothy 2:24 *The Lord's bond-servant must not be quarrelsome, but be kind to all, able to teach, patient when wronged,*	

By reading the verses above, we may reach a few conclusions about kindness. It is very clear that kindness is to be shown to all people whether they are deserving of it or not. The Bible abounds in examples of God's kindness toward us. If we are to be like Him, we must be kind as He is kind. Another conclusion can be drawn in that kindness is given for many purposes, one of which is salvation. Kindness benefits others — salvation being the biggest benefit. For those teachers and parents out there kindness is essential. For those in ministry it is basically a pre-requisite. In the Old and New Testaments mention is made of good and bad shepherds. One qualification of good shepherds is kindness. Bad shepherds were described as wolves. Wolves do not seek the best in others, but rather are self-seeking, scattering the flock, not protecting, preserving and benefiting it.

We start each day with a pocketful of benefits. We need to be on the lookout to empty our pockets by day's end.

Perhaps these final words will also inspire us to be a kind person!

Quotes

Tolstoy, the great Russian writer, was passing along a street one day when a begger stopped him and pleaded for alms. The great Russian searched through his pockets for a coin, but finding none he regretfully said, "Please don't be angry with me, my brother, but I have nothing with me. If I did I would gladly give it to you." The beggar's face flamed up, and he said, "You have given me more than I asked for. You have called me brother." — Evangelistic Illustration

It is said that when Mrs. Booth, who even more than her husband, was the life of the Salvation Army, was a little girl, running along the road with hoop and stick, she saw a prisoner dragged away by a constable to the lockup. A mob was hooting at the unfortunate culprit, and his utter loneliness appealed at once to her heart. It seemed to her that he had not a friend in the world. Quick as thought she sprang to his side and marched down the street with him, determined that he should know that there was one soul that felt for him whether he suffered for his own fault or that of another.

Who has not been thrilled by Beethoven's "Moonlight Sonata?" It is a master interpretation in sound of the unspeakable glory of a moonlit night. This beautiful piece of music was created because the composer wanted to give something of himself and his talent to a blind girl. This lady could not see the beauties of a moonlit night: blind was she to the silver sheen on trees and shrub and grass; blind was she to the silver covering on the lake; blind was she to the world of milky white in the sky. So the thoughtful and selfless Beethoven put his genius to work. He would tell her not merely in words, but in sound, of the beauty her eyes could not behold. As a result the world has been enriched. He gave the best of his talent in a selfless act of kindness. – Tonne

Lord Palmerston, Queen Victoria's Prime Minister, was crossing Westminster Bridge when a little girl ahead dropped a jug of milk. The jug broke into fragments, and she dissolved into tears. Palmerston, having no money with him dried her eyes by telling her that if she came to the same spot next day at that hour he would pay for both jug and milk. The following morning, in the midst of a cabinet meeting, he suddenly remembered his promise to the little girl, left the bewildered ministers, dashed across the bridge, popped half a crown into the waiting child's hand and hurried back. — All Nations Missionary Review

Many years ago Dwight W. Morrow, the father of Anne Lindbergh, told a group of friends that Calvin Coolidge had real presidential possibilities. They disagreed, saying that Coolidge was too quiet, and lacked color and political personality. "No one would like him," objected one of the group. But up piped little Anne, then aged six: "I like Mr. Coolidge." Then she displayed a finger with a bit of adhesive tape on it. "He was the only one who asked me about my sore finger." Mr. Morrow nodded. "There's your answer," he said.

The teacher asked the pupils to tell the meaning of loving-kindness. A little boy jumped up and said, "Well, if I was hungry and someone gave me a piece of bread that would be kindness. But if they put a little jam on it, that would be loving-kindness."

To ease another's heartache is to forget one's own. — Abraham Lincoln

XOgesis

Annie: "How is your Bible study on kindness coming?"

Ned: "Well it's a one-of-a-kind study, but it's kind of hard to figure out the kind of kindness I am the kind for, but I know I'll benefit in kind."

Annie: "Huh?"

Ned: "It's going well. Kind of you to ask."

From KJ & Friends ™ © 2010 by G Doulos

Old Testament Examples [Gen 39] [Psalm 106:7]

Describe how the LORD displays ***Kindness*** in these passages.

Describe how the LORD has been ***Kind*** to you and/or someone that you know.

List a way you will be ***Kind*** this week. Prepare a concise teaching on ***Kindness***.

My Application:

My Lesson Plan

Extra Credit – Pick any of the 10 commandments and think about how being ***Kind*** will help you fulfill the commandment.

CHARACTERISTIC OF LOVE

Discussion

Now that we have the first two positive characteristics down, we start a series of negative characteristics. These are actions that we should avoid if we are to emulate the love of God. This is similar to the Ten Commandments, where we have actions to perform, and actions to avoid. Inherent in an action to avoid is an action to take its place. As Jesus points out, it is not enough not to murder someone in order to fulfill the sixth commandment. We should pray for those we consider enemies, "turn the other cheek," and avoid calling them names or thinking ill of them. In the same way, we will discover some positive things we can do instead of not being jealous, not bragging, not being arrogant, etc. We want to go on the offensive to promote love instead of just trying to suppress bad actions. Let us now look at jealousy.

Both the Hebrew and the Greek words for being jealous can more aptly be translated as *being zealous*. The Greek verb translated as *to be jealous* even sounds like zealous, ζηλόω (*zēloō*). Being zealous, however, has its good side and its bad side. Think of being zealous or exhibiting zeal as a single-minded focus on an object, cause, person, etc. The Old Testament often refers to God as a jealous God. In fact a better translation would be that God is a zealous God, since jealousy has a negative connotation. However, let us dive into the definition of jealous and perhaps we can see how jealousy can be a good thing as well as a bad thing.

We can define jealousy as anger or fear that others will take what we have. Couple this definition with what we have stated about zeal as being a single-minded devotion and we can clearly see how God can be both zealous and jealous over His children. God zealously protects His children from bad influences, because He is concerned (jealous), that the *enemy* will lead them astray from the blessings of the Promised Land. So that is what being zealous or exhibiting *good* jealousy is about. Another great example is when Jesus chased the money changers and profiteers from the temple area. His single-minded devotion to His Father's house moved him to remove anything that would bring dishonor to His Father. He fulfilled the scripture:

Psalm 69:9 *For zeal for Your house has consumed me, And the reproaches of those who reproach You have fallen on me.*

Now let us look at the *bad* side of jealousy. It is interesting to note that many of the modern translations translate *zēloō* as *to envy*, instead of *to be jealous*. This has to do with the blending of the terms in our modern usage. Let us look at *Merriam-Webster's* definitions for jealous and envy.

Jealous is defined as: *intolerant of rivalry or unfaithfulness; hostile toward a rival or one believed to enjoy an advantage and; vigilant in guarding a possession*. Envy is defined as: *painful or resentful awareness of an advantage enjoyed by another joined with a desire to possess the same advantage and; an object of envious notice or feeling.*

The Theological Wordbook of the Old Testament has a good comparison of the two as follows: *It may prove helpful to think of "zeal" as the original sense from which derived the notions:*

"zeal for another's property" ="envy"
and "zeal for one's own property" = "jealousy."

Or still another simplistic view of the two:

Envy = Anger / Resentment that others have what we want
Jealousy = Anger / Fear others will take what we have

It is clear from the above that many situations exist where both definitions will fit. Also we can see how covetousness (the Tenth Commandment) would be a subset of envy. There is one thing that is common to both jealousy and envy. Feelings of hostility and resentment are present toward another person. So what is the root cause? What positive action(s) can we take so that we will not be jealous? Let us look at the following scriptures:

God's Zeal Toward Us	
Nahum 1:2 *A jealous and avenging God is the Lord; The Lord is avenging and wrathful. The Lord takes vengeance on His adversaries, And He reserves wrath for His enemies.*	1 Corinthians 12:6,7 *There are varieties of effects, but the same God who works all things in all persons. But to each one is given the manifestation of the Spirit for the common good.*
Luke 10:17-21 *The seventy returned with joy, saying, "Lord, even the demons are subject to us in Your name." And He said to them, "I was watching Satan fall from heaven like lightning. "Behold, I have given you authority to tread on serpents and scorpions, and over all the power of the enemy, and nothing will injure you. "Nevertheless do not rejoice in this, that the spirits are subject to you, but rejoice that your names are recorded in heaven." At that very time He rejoiced greatly in the Holy Spirit, and said, "I praise You, O Father, Lord of heaven and earth, that You have hidden these things from the wise and intelligent and have revealed them to infants. Yes, Father, for this way was well-pleasing in Your sight."*	Exodus 34:24 *For I will drive out nations before you and enlarge your borders, and no man shall covet your land when you go up three times a year to appear before the Lord your God.*

God Forbids Our Jealousy / Envy / Covetousness	
Luke 9:49-50 *John answered and said, "Master, we saw someone casting out demons in Your name; and we tried to prevent him because he does not follow along with us." But Jesus said to him, "Do not hinder him; for he who is not against you is for you."*	Deuteronomy 7:25 *The graven images of their gods you are to burn with fire; you shall not covet the silver or the gold that is on them, nor take it for yourselves, or you will be snared by it, for it is an abomination to the Lord your God.*
Job 5:2 *For anger slays the foolish man, And jealousy kills the simple.*	James 3:16 *For where jealousy and selfish ambition exist, there is disorder and every evil thing.*
Proverbs 23:17 *Do not let your heart envy sinners, But live in the fear of the Lord always.*	Deuteronomy 5:21 *You shall not covet your neighbor's wife, and you shall not desire your neighbor's house, his field or his male servant or his female servant, his ox or his donkey or anything that belongs to your neighbor.*

Examples of Our Zeal Toward Others	
Numbers 25:11 *Phinehas the son of Eleazar, the son of Aaron the priest, has turned away My wrath from the sons of Israel in that he was jealous with My jealousy among them, so that I did not destroy the sons of Israel in My jealousy.*	2 Corinthians 11:2 *For I am jealous for you with a godly jealousy; for I betrothed you to one husband, so that to Christ I might present you as a pure virgin.*
Hebrews 10:24 *and let us consider how to stimulate one another to love and good deeds,*	Numbers 11:29 *But Moses said to him, "Are you jealous for my sake? Would that all the Lord's people were prophets, that the Lord would put His Spirit upon them!"*

It is clear that God is zealous for us. He wants us to be protected from bad influences so that we can follow his Word and flourish. Then we can use our God-given gifts for His glory. So, how can we single-handedly stop coveting, envying, and being jealous? We can prevent their growth in us if we are zealous about ourselves and others in the same way God is zealous about us.

If we think about it, all three of the above-mentioned *badnesses* (not sure that is even a word) are caused by thinking that God has not sufficiently provided for us. We create this wrong thinking by comparing ourselves to others. God's provision includes material things as well as gifts and talents. We can envy someone's possessions, even where they were born. We can also envy their skills, their knowledge, their looks, their popularity, etc.

So to eliminate jealousy, envy and covetousness, our eyes must be focused on God, our hearts must be content and thankful for what He has given us, and we must serve Him with what we are and what we have.

If we are content with what He has given us, and are using it wisely (remember the parable of the talents – Matthew 25:14-30), then comparisons to others are useless and really serve no purpose. And in fact, once we get a handle on this, we will also be able to spot those people who perhaps have little or no self-esteem because they are comparing themselves when they should be sharing themselves.

There will always be people who try to make us envious and jealous. But, if we are zealous for God, and zealous about using what He has given us to serve Him, then those people will hold no sway over us.

So we count our blessings (one by one), maximize our spiritual gifts, and look for ways to encourage others to do the same. Remember, we are the apple of God's eye.

Perhaps these final words will also inspire us to be zealous (the good kind)!

Quotes

F. B. Meyer told the following experience to a few personal friends: "It was easy," he said, "to pray for the success of G. Campbell Morgan when he was in America. But when he came back to England and took a church near to mine, it was something different. The old Adam in me was inclined to jealousy, but I got my heel upon his head, and whether I felt right toward my friend, I determined to act right." "My church gave a reception for him, and I acknowledged that if it was not necessary for me to preach Sunday evenings I would dearly love to go and hear him myself. Well, that made me feel right toward him. But just see how the dear Lord helped me out of my difficulty. There was Charles Spurgeon preaching wonderfully on the other side of me. He and Mr. Morgan were so popular, and drew such crowds, that our church caught the overflow, and we had all we could accommodate." — Ministers' Research Service

The counselors of Florence asked Leonardo da Vinci, then Italy's most celebrated artist, to submit sketches for the decorations of the grand hall at Florence. One of the counselors had heard of a young and little-known artist who had done good work, Michelangelo, and asked him to submit sketches also. The sketches of Leonardo were superb, in keeping with his genius, but when the counselors saw the sketches of Michelangelo there was a spontaneous expression of wonder and enthusiasm. News of this reached Leonardo. He also heard that one of the counselors had said, "Leonardo is getting old." He was never able to get over the eclipse of his fame by Michelangelo, and the remaining years of his life were clouded with gloom and sorrow.
— C. E. Macartney

The man who keeps busy helping the man below him won't have time to envy the man above him—and there may not be anybody above him anyway.
— Henrietta C. Mears

XOgesis

KJ: “Hey, Annie, have you heard of a story written by some guy named Asap, where a dog has a piece of meat in his mouth...”

Annie: “Yeah. By the way, it’s Aesop.”

KJ: “anyway, this dog is crossing a stream, sees his reflection and thinks it’s another dog and starts barking ‘cause he wants the other dog’s meat...”

Annie: “ ...and when he barks, the meat in his mouth falls out and floats away.”

KJ: “Yeah. My mom says there is something called a moral in that story. She says a moral is a good lesson that teaches you right from wrong.”

Annie: “There are lots of good morals in that story like, be content with what you have, don’t be jealous or envious of what others have...”

KJ: “... and don’t talk with your mouth full!”

From KJ & Friends ™ © 2010 by G Doulos

OLD TESTAMENT EXAMPLES [Isaiah 37:30-35] [Psalm 69]

Describe how the LORD displays ***Zeal*** in these passages

Describe how the LORD has been ***Zealous*** for you and/or someone that you know.

List a way you will be ***Zealous*** this week. Prepare a concise teaching on combating ***Jealousy***.

My Application:

My Lesson Plan

Extra Credit – Pick any of the 10 commandments and think about how not being ***Jealous*** will help you fulfill the commandment.

CHARACTERISTIC OF LOVE

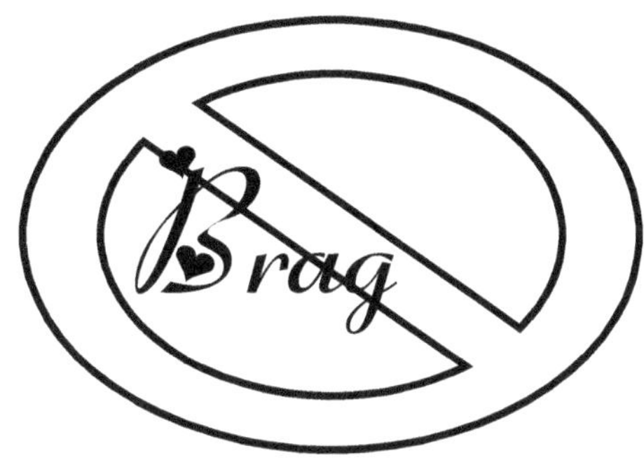

Discussion

The word used in the Greek here for *brag*, περπερεύεται (*perpereuetai*), basically means *to brag* or *boast* and has as its noun form the meaning, *braggart*. In *Vincent's Word Studies in the New Testament*, this word is defined as, *used of one who sounds his own praises. Merriam-Webster's Collegiate Dictionary* echoes this: *to talk boastfully,* and to *engage in self-glorification*. The Greek has a separate word for boasting. Boasting is something that can be good or bad, and the boast may not necessarily be about one's own accomplishments.

Boasting in things other than ourselves can be quite beneficial, as the apostle Paul says:

1 Corinthians 1:27-31 *but God has chosen the foolish things of the world to shame the wise, and God has chosen the weak things of the world to shame the things which are strong, and the base things of the world and the despised God has chosen, the things that are not, so that He may nullify the things that are, so that no man may boast before God. But by His doing you are in Christ Jesus, who became to us wisdom from God, and righteousness and sanctification, and redemption, so that, just as it is written, "Let him who boasts, boast in the Lord."*

But the word (περπερεύεται) used here for bragging makes it clear that this is not *good* boasting. It literally means *being a braggart*. It means that our boasting is about our self. The timing of this characteristic of love following *do not be jealous* is perfect. Let us follow the train of thought. We are commanded not to be covetous or envious about another person's property, skills or achievements. This will create ill feelings and prevent us from having good relationships with others. It may also make us feel bad and promote a low self-esteem within us. Now, what happens when we brag about ourselves, our property, our skills, and our achievements? It tempts people to be jealous, and envious, and covetous of us. It may contribute to their having a low self-esteem. It is putting a stumbling block in front of others that is entirely unnecessary.

We as zealous Christians want to encourage others to use the gifts and talents that God has given to them. We do not want to try and make them feel bad that they are not as successful as we are with our gifts and talents. Bragging does not elevate others; it puts them down, as we seek to elevate ourselves above them. To put it succinctly, we are commanded to not be jealous of others, and to not cause jealousy in others. We are commanded to not be envious of others, and to not cause envy in others by our bragging.

So what is the correct way to handle acknowledging our accomplishments? How can we prevent ourselves from being a braggart? Let us look at the following scriptures:

God Boasts on Us	
Matthew 19:28,29 *And Jesus said to them, "Truly I say to you, that you who have followed Me, in the regeneration when the Son of Man will sit on His glorious throne, you also shall sit upon twelve thrones, judging the twelve tribes of Israel. And everyone who has left houses or brothers or sisters or father or mother 1or children or farms for My name's sake, will receive many times as much, and will inherit eternal life."*	Luke 10:41,42 *But the Lord answered and said to her, "Martha, Martha, you are worried and bothered about so many things; but only one thing is necessary, for Mary has chosen the good part, which shall not be taken away from her."*
Matthew 8:10 *Now when Jesus heard this, He marveled and said to those who were following, "Truly I say to you, I have not found such great faith with anyone in Israel."*	Isaiah 43:4 *Since you are precious in My sight, Since you are honored and I love you, I will give other men in your place and other peoples in exchange for your life.*

God Requests Us to not Brag	
Matthew 6:3-4 *But when you give to the poor, do not let your left hand know what your right hand is doing, so that your giving will be in secret; and your Father who sees what is done in secret will reward you.*	Judges 7:2 *The Lord said to Gideon, "The people who are with you are too many for Me to give Midian into their hands, for Israel would become boastful, saying, 'My own power has delivered me.'"*
Proverbs 27:2 *Let another praise you, and not your own mouth; A stranger, and not your own lips.*	Galatians 5:26 *Let us not become boastful, challenging one another, envying one another.*
Jeremiah 9:23,24 *Thus says the Lord, "Let not a wise man boast of his wisdom, and let not the mighty man boast of his might, let not a rich man boast of his riches; but let him who boasts boast of this, that he understands and knows Me, that I am the Lord who exercises lovingkindness, justice and righteousness on earth; for I delight in these things," declares the Lord.*	

Examples of Our Good Boasting	
Psalm 20:7 *Some boast in chariots and some in horses, But we will boast in the name of the Lord, our God.*	Psalm 34:2 *My soul will make its boast in the Lord; The humble will hear it and rejoice.*
2 Corinthians 7:4 *Great is my confidence in you; great is my boasting on your behalf. I am filled with comfort; I am overflowing with joy in all our affliction.*	2 Corinthians 12:9 *And He has said to me, "My grace is sufficient for you, for power is perfected in weakness." Most gladly, therefore, I will rather boast about my weaknesses, so that the power of Christ may dwell in me.*

From the verses above it is clear that we can boast in the Lord and boast on others. It is also clear that the Lord is very proud of us. He will always have great things to say about any and all of our victories and sacrifices for His sake. Remember this always.

The Lord will always be our greatest source of encouragement. He wants us to succeed. He loves us and loves to boast about us to the angels. Remember Job. God really thought he was amazing. Job had his faults, but he was dearly loved.

So how do we handle speaking about our own accomplishments? Well this one is easy — just be quiet about it. Do not be a show-off. The Bible is extremely clear on this. Two things to remember: Let others recount our victories, and we should not let our left hand know what our right hand is doing. We will explain that one a little further.

On the surface of Matthew 6:3,4 (see above verses) we may wonder how we can do one thing with one hand that the other hand may not even know about. We can assume that this is an expression emphasizing that we should do good things without expecting anyone to give us any credit; and that it would be done in such secrecy that we would not be aware of it if that were possible. This would be a reasonable assumption and recent discoveries in how the brain functions make this verse quite an interesting statement. Scientists have relatively recently discovered that different parts of the brain control different parts of the body.

And you guessed it, the left hand and the right hand are in fact controlled by different sides of the brain. The left hand is controlled by the right side of the brain and the right hand is controlled by the left side of the brain. The left side of the brain tends to manage our verbal, analytical, rational, logical sides, while the right side of the brain runs our nonverbal, synthetic, non-rational, and intuitive sides. Thus the more we dwell on our accomplishments the more we engage both sides of our brain, and allow the left and right sides of the brain to fully know what we have done. If we spend almost no time thinking about how *great* we are, or what we have done, then perhaps only one side of our brain will truly know what we have done. Perhaps then truly the one hand will not know what the other has done.

From a practical standpoint this is really not that possible, but you get the idea. The less time we dwell on our past accomplishments the better for us. God will make sure we are encouraged. Count on it. It is better that others praise us anyway. If someone praises us for something we did in the past, we should always be gracious and say *thank you*. We can rejoice in our victories each day, but as a new day dawns we have a big zero on our good deeds list. So at the start of each day we should start out by boasting in the Lord and in others, and not dwell on our past deeds.

Looking at this in another way it may appear that the antidote for stopping jealousy and bragging may be the exact opposite of each other. Let us compare and contrast these.

For envy / jealousy *the cure* is to not to compare ourselves to others, but rather be zealous in our attention to using our gifts and talents to serve the Lord. For bragging *the cure* is to think of others rather than ourselves and boast in them and build them up, and not think too highly of our gifts, talents and accomplishments as we serve the Lord. Remember that measuring and comparing ourselves to others invariably leads to either envy / jealousy or bragging.

Jealousy and envy try to bring others down to our level, while bragging tries to bring us up to what we perceive is the level of others or beyond. In both cases, where we are in relationship to another person is completely unimportant. All that matters is our walk with God. The only measure we need to worry about is the distance between us and the Lord. The question we can ask at the close of every day, *Are we closer to or farther away from the Lord?* Remember, let other people praise us, and let us not be too enamored with our good deeds. We should concentrate on praising the accomplishments of others. We will close with one additional verse from the Lord Jesus Christ.

Luke 17:10 *So you too, when you do all the things which are commanded you, say, 'We are unworthy slaves; we have done only that which we ought to have done.'*

Perhaps these final words will also inspire us to refrain from bragging but concentrate on proper boasting!

Quotes

In basic training, our first sergeant made things very clear. He told us, "Don't question anything I say or tell you to do. Don't worry—I hardly ever make mistakes. Matter of fact, I've made only one mistake in my life. I once thought I was wrong about something. It turned out I wasn't." — Dalex J. LeBlanc

A minister who was walking along a road saw a crowd of boys surrounding a dog. "What are you doing with the dog?" asked the kindly minister. "Whoever tells the biggest lie, he wins the dog." "Oh, my, my, my," exclaimed the minister, "when I was a little boy like you here I never told a lie." There was a moment's silence. "Here," said one of the little fellows, "you win the dog."

We always weaken whatever we exaggerate. — Jean Francois De Laharpe

Few people need voice lessons to sing their own praise. — E. C. Mckenzie

Do you wish men to speak well of you? Then never speak well of yourself. — Pascual

If a fish escapes, it was a big one. — Malay Proverb

Sign in front of an Atlanta restaurant featuring fried chicken: "If the Colonel Had Our Chicken Recipe He'd Be a General." — Atlanta Journal

XOgesis

Annie: "Thanks for the loan of a dollar but why are you giving it to me with your left hand behind your back?"

KJ: "This way my left hand doesn't know what my right hand is doing so I won't become a braggart!"

Annie: "Does that work?"

KJ: "Yeah! Yesterday I gave $2 away with my right hand, before that I accepted a trophy with my left hand, then I washed the dishes with only my right hand, was a bit difficult, but I did great, then before that with only one hand I beat someone in doing push ups, then before that..."

Annie: "So this is not bragging ??? I think one of your hands must be peeking!"

OLD TESTAMENT EXAMPLES [Job 1:8] [Judges 7 and 8]

Describe how the LORD displays *good* ***Boasting*** or prevents us from ***Bragging,*** in these passages.

Describe how the LORD has been ***Boasting*** on you and/or someone that you know.

List a way you will ***Boast*** (good***)*** this week. Prepare a concise teaching on combating ***Bragging***.

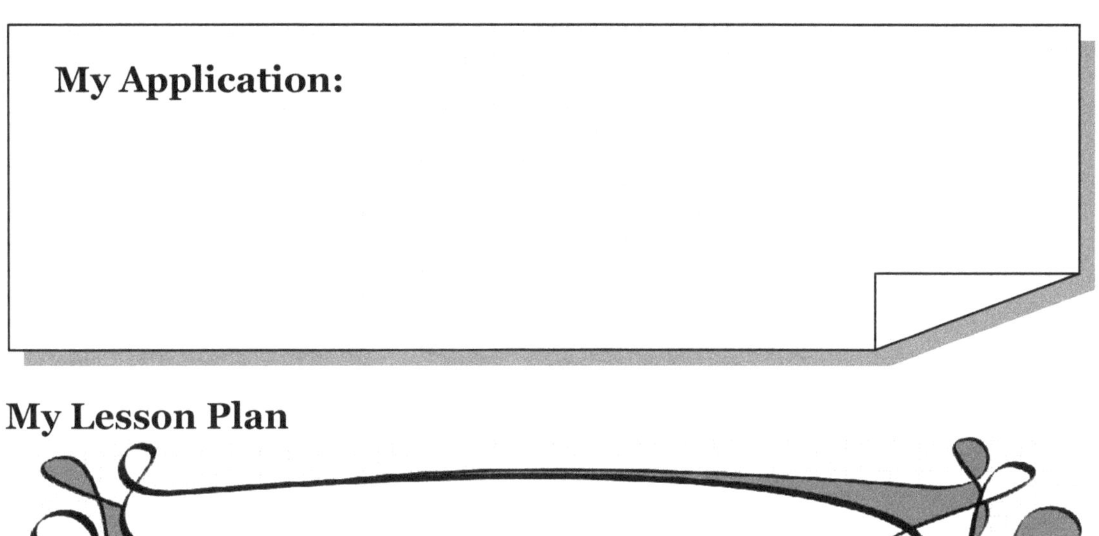

My Lesson Plan

Extra Credit – Pick any of the 10 commandments and think about how not ***Bragging*** will help you fulfill the commandment.

CHARACTERISTIC OF LOVE

Discussion

The word used in the Greek here for *arrogant*, φυσιοῦται (*phusioutai*), basically means *to be arrogant* or *proud.* In *Vincent's Word Studies in the New Testament,* this word is defined as *to be puffed up* and it is used only by the apostle Paul in the books of Corinthians and Colossians. It may be derived from another Greek word φῦσα (*phusa*), meaning *a pair of bellows. Merriam-Webster's Collegiate Dictionary* echoes this, saying, *exaggerating or disposed to exaggerate one's own worth or importance in an overbearing manner.*

While bragging as previously discussed may boast of many deeds, arrogance is more an attitude that inflates our self-worth out of proportion. It can be argued that a janitor of a school and the principal of a school are jobs differing in value. However, both the janitor and the principal can still be arrogant. It is not the job or position that makes us arrogant but our perspective on our worth compared to others. There is that same problem again!! Comparing ourselves — aaghh!! Arrogance also has to do with the thought that we do not need others. Not only are the arrogant more lofty in their estimation of themselves, but they convince themselves that they do not need what others can give because they undervalue (even dismiss) the contributions of others.

So how does one become arrogant? What does God say about it? What is the remedy? Perhaps we can start with the opposite of arrogance, which would be humility. Let's compare the two.

Merriam-Webster's Collegiate Dictionary displays the following information about the word *humble*.

Humble
[Middle English, from Old French, from Latin humilis low, humble, from humus earth; akin to Greek chthōn earth, chamai on the ground] (13th century)
1 : not proud or haughty : not arrogant or assertive 2 : reflecting, expressing, or offered in a spirit of deference or submission ⟨a humble apology⟩ 3 a: ranking low in a hierarchy or scale : insignificant, unpretentious b: not costly or luxurious ⟨a humble contraption⟩

So if we compare the lowliness of the humble being akin to the humus of the earth, to the inflated (by bellows) position of the arrogant, we see the stark contrast of these two individuals. Most people start somewhere in between these two levels. So how do we lower ourselves to obtain true humility; and conversely, how do we inflate ourselves to become arrogant and full of pride? Start with the verses below, and then read on.

<table>
<tr><th colspan="2">God's View of Arrogance</th></tr>
<tr><td colspan="2">James 3:13-18 Who among you is wise and understanding? Let him show by his good behavior his deeds in the gentleness of wisdom. But if you have bitter jealousy and selfish ambition in your heart, do not be arrogant and so lie against the truth. This wisdom is not that which comes down from above, but is earthly, natural, demonic. For where jealousy and selfish ambition exist, there is disorder and every evil thing. But the wisdom from above is first pure, then peaceable, gentle, reasonable, full of mercy and good fruits, unwavering, without hypocrisy. And the seed whose fruit is righteousness is sown in peace by those who make peace.</td></tr>
<tr><td>1 Corinthians 8:1 Now concerning things sacrificed to idols, we know that we all have knowledge. Knowledge makes arrogant, but love edifies.</td><td>1 Corinthians 1:27, but God has chosen the foolish things of the world to shame the wise, and God has chosen the weak things of the world to shame the things which are strong,</td></tr>
<tr><td>Proverbs 14:16 A wise man is cautious and turns away from evil, But a fool is arrogant and careless.</td><td>Proverbs 28:25 An arrogant man stirs up strife, But he who trusts in the Lord will prosper.</td></tr>
</table>

<table>
<tr><th colspan="2">God Requests Us to Not be Arrogant</th></tr>
<tr><td>Ezekiel 16:49 Behold, this was the guilt of your sister Sodom: she and her daughters had arrogance, abundant food and careless ease, but she did not help the poor and needy.</td><td>Obadiah 1:3 The arrogance of your heart has deceived you, You who live in the clefts of the rock, In the loftiness of your dwelling place, Who say in your heart, 'Who will bring me down to earth?'</td></tr>
<tr><td colspan="2">1 Corinthians 4:5-7 Therefore do not go on passing judgment before the time, but wait until the Lord comes who will both bring to light the things hidden in the darkness and disclose the motives of men's hearts; and then each man's praise will come to him from God. Now these things, brethren, I have figuratively applied to myself and Apollos for your sakes, so that in us you may learn not to exceed what is written, so that no one of you will become arrogant in behalf of one against the other. For who regards you as superior? What do you have that you did not receive? And if you did receive it, why do you boast as if you had not received it?</td></tr>
</table>

Examples of Our Humility Towards Others	
Matthew 19:13,14 *Then some children were brought to Him so that He might lay His hands on them and pray; and the disciples rebuked them. But Jesus said, "Let the children alone, and do not hinder them from coming to Me; for the kingdom of heaven belongs to such as these."*	1 Peter 5:5 *"You younger men, likewise, be subject to your elders; and all of you, clothe yourselves with humility toward one another, for God is opposed to the proud, but gives grace to the humble.*
Romans 12:3-5 *For through the grace given to me I say to everyone among you not to think more highly of himself than he ought to think; but to think so as to have sound judgment, as God has allotted to each a measure of faith. For just as we have many members in one body and all the members do not have the same function, so we, who are many, are one body in Christ, and individually members one of another.*	Ephesians 5:22, 25 *"Wives, be subject to your own husbands, as to the Lord.* *Husbands, love your wives, just as Christ also loved the church and gave Himself up for her,* Ephesians 6:5,9 *Slaves, be obedient to those who are your masters according to the flesh, with fear and trembling, in the sincerity of your heart, as to Christ;* *And masters, do the same things to them, and give up threatening, knowing that both their Master and yours is in heaven, and there is no partiality with Him.*

We have listed some observations about arrogance from the above verses. Let us see if we can figure out how one inflates this monster.

Arrogant traits	Humble traits
know it all	reasonable
bitter jealousy	peacemaker
selfish ambition	full of mercy
lying	without hypocrisy
disorderly	unwavering
stirs up strife	gentle
pride	peaceable
boasting	righteous
deceived by pride	good fruits

Without going into too much analysis a couple of thoughts are offered. Arrogance is characterized by self-glorification and results in the destruction of people, plans and purposes, through strife, disorder, bitter jealousy, etc. Humility, however is contrasted in that it seeks not glory for itself; rather, it promotes the well-being of others and results in the continual growth of people, plans and purposes through gentle, peaceful, unwavering, and righteous behavior. The results or effects of the two are in stark contrast to each other.

Perhaps we can picture the difference between these contrasting qualities by reflecting on people in the Bible who had these traits. Moses was the most humble man in the Bible. Though he had his faults, he was highly esteemed by God. No one else could have possibly done a better job leading thousands of people through the wilderness, while patiently teaching, encouraging and admonishing everyone about the ways of the Lord. John the Baptist spent his whole life preparing people to receive salvation from the Messiah who was to come. And then at the height of his ministry, he simply said, *He must increase, and I must decrease.* He gradually faded into the background, until he was murdered by King Herod. We could go on about others, such as King David, who in true humility waited until the Lord had dealt with Saul before he assumed the reins of his kingdom.

The arrogant folks in the Bible would include the likes of Cain, Pharaoh, and King Saul. So how did these folks become arrogant? By looking at a few episodes of their lives we can get an inkling of how this might have occurred. The next time we read the books Genesis and First and Second Samuel we should keep this in mind.

Perhaps these final words will also inspire us to refrain from being arrogant and concentrate on being humble!

Quotes

A rich man once invited many honored guests for a feast. His own chair, richly decorated, was placed at one end of the long table. While he was away, each guest seated himself according to his own esteem of his position in sight of the master. When time came and all were seated, the master moved his chair to the other end of the table!

One of Spurgeon's students went into a pulpit with every expression of confidence but he had an extremely difficult time. He came down distressed, almost brokenhearted, and he went to Spurgeon about it. The words of Spurgeon to him were these, "If you had gone up as you came down, you would have come down as you went up." — Al Bryant

XOgesis

KJ: "I was elected class president today, and that goofy old Richard was elected as vice-president. Why do you need a vice-president anyway? The president is the one who makes all the decisions. My first action as president will be to abolish all the other lesser positions like vice-president, secretary, and ..."

Ned: "You do know they will have a vote on that action."

KJ: "What?! I guess my first action will have to be to abolish voting rights for everyone except me."

Ned: "But they will have a vote on that, too."

KJ: "Oh well I guess I am stuck with them. Being president is turning out to be harder than I thought."

From KJ & Friends ™ © 2010 by G Doulos

OLD TESTAMENT EXAMPLES [Gen 19:1-22]

Describe how the LORD has shown ***Humility*** or dealt with the ***Arrogant*** in this passage.

Describe how the LORD has shown ***Humility*** toward you and/or someone that you know or has dealt with your ***Arrogance***.

List a way you will show ***Humility*** this week. Prepare a concise teaching on combating ***Arrogance***.

My Application:

My Lesson Plan

Extra Credit – Pick any of the 10 commandments and think about how being ***Humble*** will help you fulfill the commandment.

CHARACTERISTIC OF LOVE

Discussion

The word used in the Greek here for *acting unbecomingly,* ἀσχημονεῖ (*aschēmonei*), basically means *to act indecently, to be rude* or *to behave in a disgraceful or shameful manner*. The word in the Greek has a negative prefix *a,* which is negating the word *schēmonei,* that can be translated as *form, conduct,* or *character*. So literally translated it means *without character*. Depending on the degree of our actions when we act unbecomingly, people may say that we are not conducting ourselves well or our behavior is downright shameful and disgraceful. To act unbecomingly is to not care about our reputation or our character. Once we cease to worry about conducting ourselves properly, any lewd, degrading or shameful actions are open to tempt us. We want to be an example of decency not indecency. We want to be known as a decent person.

There are a variety of examples in the New Testament on this character quality. We will look at these one at a time. Read the verses that follow.

1 Corinthians 7:36,37 *If anyone thinks he is acting improperly toward the virgin he is engaged to, and if she is getting along in years and he feels he ought to marry, he should do as he wants. He is not sinning. They should get married. But the man who has settled the matter in his own mind, who is under no compulsion but has control over his own will, and who has made up his mind not to marry the virgin—this man also does the right thing.* (NIV)

The word *improperly* used in this New International Version (NIV) of the verse is the Greek word *aschēmonein* (translated as *unbecomingly* in the NASB95). The connotation based on this particular context is that the improper behavior is of a physical or sensual nature. This is one characteristic of indecent behavior. When we are not in control of our sensual passions it may lead to behavior that is indecent. It is indecent to want to satisfy our own desires at the expense of others.

Another use of this word for indecent (*shame*) is found in the following verses:

Jude 12,13 *These are the men who are hidden reefs in your love feasts when they feast with you without fear, caring for themselves; clouds without water, carried along by winds; autumn trees without fruit, doubly dead, uprooted; wild waves of the sea, casting up their own shame like foam; wandering stars, for whom the black darkness has been reserved forever.*

The people being described here pretend to be believers who attend *love feasts,* which may represent church fellowships gathering over a meal. These pretenders (*trees without fruit*) care only for themselves and display their shameful behavior like foam on the sea. Sea foam is composed of many things including wastes from plants and fish and other things that are decomposing. This includes the dregs on the sea floor that get churned up to the top of the water.

So the illustration is a great one. Wastes and foul-smelling objects are disgraceful and distasteful and should be kept buried or even incinerated. But in this case these indecent things are actually on display. Such is one characteristic of an indecent person: not caring if what is deemed indecent is on display.

An Old Testament verse that conveys indecent behavior is found in Ezekiel.

Ezekiel 23:29 *They will deal with you in hatred, take all your property, and leave you naked and bare. And the nakedness of your harlotries will be uncovered, both your lewdness and your harlotries.*

In this verse and in Ezekiel chapters sixteen and twenty-three, indecent behavior is related to being naked or nakedness, which is used as a metaphor for indecent behavior. Again the message is clear. It is not appropriate to go around naked or view nakedness in others (e.g., the episode of Ham and Noah, Genesis 9:22,23).

One final verse on this topic:

Ephesians 5:3,4 *But immorality or any impurity or greed must not even be named among you, as is proper among saints; and there must be no filthiness and silly talk, or coarse jesting, which are not fitting, but rather giving of thanks.*

The specific indecent behavior mentioned is when we talk about indecent things. The three words sum up indecent talking very well: filthiness, silly talk and coarse jesting.

So we see that indecent behavior can be what we do ourselves, how we behave with others, and what we talk about. Indecency can be mild but also can be horrible. An easy way to remember this is that indecent behavior encompasses the following actions: *rude, crude and lewd.*

Thus while lewd behavior is indecent and can get us arrested, rude behavior is also indecent and will arrest our good reputation and testimony for Christ. Let us now look at the following additional scriptures.

God's View of Being Indecent	
Deuteronomy 23:14 *Since the LORD your God walks in the midst of your camp to deliver you and to defeat your enemies before you, therefore your camp must be holy; and He must not see anything indecent among you or He will turn away from you.*	*Isaiah 47:3 Your nakedness will be uncovered, Your shame also will be exposed; I will take vengeance and will not spare a man.*
Romans 1:27 and in the same way also the men abandoned the natural function of the woman and burned in their desire toward one another, men with men committing indecent acts and receiving in their own persons the due penalty of their error.	

God Requests Us to Not be Indecent	
Ephesians 4:29 Let no unwholesome word proceed from your mouth, but only such a word as is good for edification according to the need of the moment, so that it will give grace to those who hear.	*1 Timothy 2:9,10 Likewise, I want women to adorn themselves with proper clothing, modestly and discreetly, not with braided hair and gold or pearls or costly garments, but rather by means of good works, as is proper for women making a claim to godliness.*

Examples of Our Decent Behavior Toward Others	
Gen 9:23 *But Shem and Japheth took a garment and laid it upon both their shoulders and walked backward and covered the nakedness of their father; and their faces were turned away, so that they did not see their father's nakedness.*	Matthew 1:19 *And Joseph her husband, being a righteous man and not wanting to disgrace her, planned to send her away secretly.*

Perhaps these final words will also inspire us to refrain from acting unbecomingly and concentrate on being decent!

Quotes

In 1974, the research firm of Daniel Yankelovich, Inc., surveyed thirty-five hundred young people, ages sixteen to twenty-five. The interviews sought to learn what these selected individuals felt about "every important value" in today's world.

The study indicated that only 31 percent considered premarital sexual relations as morally wrong, compared with 52 percent in a 1969 survey. Opposition to abortion dropped from 58 percent to 45 percent in the same period. The proportion who considered "Living a clean moral life a very important value" fell from 71 percent to 52 percent. It would seem that standards are shifting into the patterns that existed in the days of Noah.
— Bible Expositor

In the United States 21% of all first babies are conceived before marriage, and 10% of all births are illegitimate. In some countries the rate is as high as 70% illegitimate.

Disney looked around for a worthy male star to play in "Mary Poppins." He settled on Dick Van Dyke—"my only choice"—when he heard that Van Dyke taught Sunday school and prayed with his children at bedtime. Disney also learned that Van Dyke had said, "I won't appear in a movie that I can't take my children to see." Van Dyke gave a great performance. The picture got thirteen Academy Award nominations.

XOgesis

Ned: “What are you looking up in the dictionary?”

KJ: “...rude, crude and socially inaccessible. Mom said that I was acting like that. I wanted to know what it meant so she said to look it up. I get that crude means doing shameful stuff, but all I get for socially inaccessible is being a hermit. Do hermits do shameful stuff?

Ned: “Yeah. Haven’t you heard about the hermit crab? If you are crabby you do shameful stuff, and a hermit crab is the worst. And remember in the book of Jude, where it says that some bad people were like *wild waves of the sea casting up their own shame like foam?* What do you think was in that sea foam? Hermit crabs of course!”

KJ: “Is that really true?”

Ned: “KJ, I’m just joking. Your mom probably said you were socially unacceptable, not inaccessible.”

KJ: “That’s a relief, because I have a pet hermit crab and he seems nice.”

Ned: “>>Sigh<<”

From KJ & Friends ™ © 2010 by G Doulos

OLD TESTAMENT EXAMPLES [Ps 25:3] [Prov 13:18] [Lev 20:26]

Describe how the LORD displays ***Decency*** or prevents us from ***Acting Unbecomingly,*** in these passages.

Describe how the LORD has been encouraging you and/or someone that you know to act ***Decently.***

List a way you will behave ***Decently*** this week. Prepare a concise teaching on ***Indecency***.

My Application:

My Lesson Plan

Extra Credit – Pick any of the 10 commandments and think about how being ***Decent*** will help you fulfill the commandment.

CHARACTERISTIC OF LOVE

Discussion

The expression used in the Greek here for *does not seek its own*, οὐ ζητεῖ τὰ ἑαυτῆς (*ou zētei ta heautēs*), is translated literally word for word as: *not — it seeks — things — of herself* (herself being our subject *Love*). It is written very generically so that we can examine all of the *things* that pertain to ourselves, to see if our seeking *these things* is preventing us from seeking those same *things* for others. It does not mean that we should not take care of ourselves. A good corollary to this would be the following verse:

Philippians 2:4, d*o not merely look out for your own personal interests, but also for the interests of others.*

This aspect of love is reminding us of the second greatest commandment:

Matthew 22:39 *The second is like it, 'You shall love your neighbor as yourself.'*

As we plan our day, our week, our year, our life, we need to ask if we are consumed with seeking those things that pertain primarily to ourselves, to our own interests, or to our own benefit.

This simple expression (*does not seek its own*) has a surprisingly wide variety of interpretative nuances as the differing Bible translations of our study text 1 Corinthians 13:5 illustrate:

NAS: *...it does not seek its own...*
NIV: *...it is not self-seeking...*
RSV: *...Love does not insist on its own way...*
NET: *...it is not self-serving...*
KJV: *...seeketh not her own...*

Paul uses a similar expression employing the same Greek words as above:

1Corinthians 10:24 *Let no one seek his own good but that of his neighbor.*

The other Bible translations are much more in-synch on this passage:

NAS: *Let no one seek his own good, but that of his neighbor.*
NIV: *Nobody should seek his own good, but the good of others.*
RSV: *Let no one seek his own good, but the good of his neighbor.*
NET: *Do not seek your own good, but the good of the other person.*
KJV: *Let no man seek his own, but every man another's wealth.*

It is very interesting that in the Greek for 1 Corinthians 10:24 the word for *good* is not actually used. The expression literally translated would be, *Let no one seek that of himself, but that of the other.* The words that the other translations use such as, *good, neighbor or wealth* are not found in the Greek. The translators picked those words to try and convey the sense of the verse. As an aside, from these simple examples we can see that sometimes translators use words that too narrowly confine the meaning of the text. Sometimes the words they choose can actually subtly change the basic meaning.

For example, the RSV for 1 Corinthians 13:5 uses *insist on its own way*. That can be confusing especially if we actually do need to insist on a way that is clearly better. The other translations better convey the meaning of not being absorbed with seeking one's own things by using words such as self-seeking or self-serving. Also, as an example, the KJV for 1 Corinthians 10:24 intimates that we are to seek to make others wealthy instead of ourselves. That is too narrow a thought and thus changes the sense of the text too much.

From these verses it is clear that the priority in life is not us. How difficult this is for some to grasp. I am not number one, I am not the most important thing, and I am not the only thing that matters.

However, the Lord knows our interests and goals in life and what we want to accomplish. He has a unique way of ensuring our success. By making our interests and goals subservient to the interest and goals of others, this will help ensure that our (God-given) goals are accomplished. This is similar to:

Matthew 6:33, *But seek first His kingdom and His righteousness, and all these things will be added to you;*

and

Matthew 10:39 *He who has found his life will lose it, and he who has lost his life for My sake will find it.*

Let us now look at the following additional scriptures:

God's View of Being Self-Centered	
Matthew 23:25 *Woe to you, scribes and Pharisees, hypocrites! For you clean the outside of the cup and of the dish, but inside they are full of robbery and self-indulgence.*	Romans 6:6 *knowing this, that our old self was crucified with Him, in order that our body of sin might be done away with, so that we would no longer be slaves to sin;*
James 3:16 *For where jealousy and selfish ambition exist, there is disorder and every evil thing.*	

God Requests Us to Not be Self-Centered	
Titus 1:7 *For the overseer must be above reproach as God's steward, not self-willed, not quick-tempered, not addicted to wine, not pugnacious, not fond of sordid gain,*	Philippians 2:3 *Do nothing from selfishness or empty conceit, but with humility of mind regard one another as more important than yourselves;*

Examples of Our Selfless Behavior Toward Others	
1 Samuel 19:1–7 Jonathan risks the ire of his father King Saul to put in a good word for David so that his father would not seek to kill David anymore. It worked this time.	1 Kings 18:3–4 *Ahab called Obadiah who was over the household. (Now Obadiah feared the* LORD *greatly; for when Jezebel destroyed the prophets of the* LORD, *Obadiah took a hundred prophets and hid them by fifties in a cave, and provided them with bread and water.)*

Perhaps these final words will also inspire us to refrain from being self-centered and concentrate on others.

Quotes

Dear Friend:

Our church membership	*1400*
Nonresident membership	*75*
Balance left to do the work...	*1325*
Elderly folks who have done their share in the past	*25*
Balance left to do the work...	*1300*
Sick and shut-in folks	*25*
Balance left to do the work...	*1275*
Membership who did not pledge	*350*
Christmas and Easter members	*300*
Balance left to do the work...	*625*
Members who are too tired and overworked	*300*
Balance left to do the work...	*325*
Alibiers	*200*
Balance left to do the work...	*125*
Members who are too busy somewhere else	*123*
Balance left to do the work...	*2*

Just you and me—and brother, you'd better get busy, for it's too much for me!
— Progress

A small boy and his sister were riding on the back of the new wooden horse given to them as a present. Suddenly the boy turned to his sister and said: "If one of us would get off there would be more room for me."

"Be Yourself!" is about the worse advice you can give to some people.

My idea of an agreeable person is one who agrees with me. – Samuel Johnson

Admiration: Our polite recognition of another person's resemblance to ourselves.

XOgesis

Ned: "KJ, why are you staring into the refrigerator?"

KJ: "I am trying to decide if I should eat the last piece of pie or let my sister have it."

Ned: "Well you should follow the golden rule, you know, do unto others, love your neighbor as yourself."

KJ: "Thanks that settles it!"

<< Later >>

Ned: "So, I bet your sister was happy you saved that piece of pie for her."

KJ: "Well, actually she was mad because I ate it. But I told her that I was following your advice."

Ned: "My advice?! What! I didn't tell you ..."

KJ: "You said love your neighbor as yourself. But she's my sister not my neighbor , so it was OK for me to eat it, 'cause I wasn't doing anything bad to my neighbor."

Ned: "But that's not what... I mean... your sister is still your... well she's ... you should of... Oh forget it!"

OLD TESTAMENT EXAMPLES [Numbers 16]

Describe how the LORD displays ***Selfless*** behavior or prevents us from being ***Self-centered,*** in this passage.

Describe how the LORD has been ***Selfless*** on your behalf and/or someone that you know.

List a way you will be ***Selfless*** this week. Prepare a concise teaching on combating ***Self-Centeredness.***

My Lesson Plan

Extra Credit – Pick any of the 10 commandments and think about how not being ***Self-Centered*** will help you fulfill the commandment.

CHARACTERISTIC OF LOVE

Discussion

The word used in the Greek here for *provoked*, παροξύνεται (*paroxunetai*), has a variety of similar meanings including*: to be spurred, urged, stimulated, provoked* or *stirred (*to anger*)*. In a similar way to boasting or being zealous, this word can have positive or negative connotations. We can spur people on to good works, or we can provoke people by doing things we know they hate. We can make somebody feel angry or indignant, provoke an argument, and yet our actions can also provoke creativity, sympathy, courage, and even bravery.

When the Bible commands us not to be provoked, the idea is that we will not allow ourselves to lose control when provoked by others. This quality of not allowing ourselves to be provoked is different then the character quality of exhibiting patience. This difference is best described by looking at different scenarios.

We use patience when we are trying to teach others new skills. Our students may take a long time to master the skill, which may try our patience, but they are certainly not trying to provoke us. On the other hand, this same student may constantly talk in class, not stand still in line, do the things that he or she knows we do not like, which will provoke us and tempt us to become very upset. Also we may like to have our class organized in a very particular way and our students may take some liberties and rearrange a few things. This will really, truly provoke us and tempt us to be very upset indeed.

Note that some provocations deserve punishment, but it must be the right punishment at the right time. We are not called to allow injustice to continue, but we are called to administer justice in the proper way. When we lose control of our emotions we may be tempted to act rashly and incorrectly. When we can take a quick breath that can allow provoking without losing our cool, it is a great asset. We can then deal properly with a given situation. We do not want to act rashly and then create a worse situation.

By not allowing ourselves to be provoked it can help us to be calm and clear and deal properly with the situation. Call it having a thick skin. Call it not having a chip on your shoulder. It is the practice of self-control. So how do we stimulate ourselves to stay above the fray and the fracas? How do we provoke ourselves to be provoke-proof? How do we become a self-controlled person, not overly sensitive and easily irritated?

First we need to examine the ways that we are provoked. We need to know our weaknesses. Not everyone is provoked in the same way. We need to separate what provocations that need to be dealt with later and those that we need to let slide. In all cases we need to handle the initial provocation with love.

As we stated above we need to separate those things that provoke us that we can tolerate to a point, and those things that should not be tolerated, but dealt with in an appropriate way.

So what are things or circumstances that provoke us but are not necessarily inherently or overtly evil? How about our pet peeves? How about all the times that we say ours is the best way and we do not want to hear another way? Certain situations or people (sometimes quite innocently) may bother us to a point where we become upset. In these cases we need to deal with ourselves, not the situation or the people. Some examples follow:

We may share an office and our co-worker may like it one temperature and we like it another. The way people drive their car may push us to the verge of road rage. We may get upset based on the weather ("rainy days and Mondays always get us down"). Arguments over our favorite subjects, people or family, may tempt us to lose it. Our children may do a lot of little things that annoy us. The common theme here is that people are doing things that we do not like or we are in situations that we do not like. It is provoking us because we do not like it when things do not go our way. In some of these cases we do not even have an opportunity to express our displeasure, which can make us even more upset. In other cases, we are being provoked by an opinion, which may not be evil or immoral, but it is different from our own, and we may not be able to hear it without being upset.

We need to employ understanding and compassion in order to keep ourselves from getting upset. We need to keep the right perspective on the situation. In some cases if we seek to understand why certain situations or other people bother us, and if we can step back or give them a break (compassion), we remove our own feelings, stubbornness and pride from the equation. What once seems so annoying to us perhaps we can now view as trivial. We have effectively dealt with the problem — us.

There are situations where the people who provoke us do actually need to be talked to, admonished, disciplined, or possibly rebuked and punished. But even in these cases, our initial reaction is not anger and vengeance, but understanding and compassion. The Old Testament abounds in examples. Even though people constantly provoked the Lord by their actions, He exhibited the same consistent compassion and understanding. He desired that they would eventually see the error of their ways and repent. He did not zap people right away but gave them room. That is our model as well. Only when it was clear that the people had no intention of repenting or had become mired in a bad habit did He administer any punishment. For those people who wanted to turn their life around, He administered any chastisement in small doses, increasing it only if needed. For those who were brazenly rebellious, the discipline was more severe and administered more often. In every case because the Lord starts with love, He is able to administer the perfect discipline to turn our lives around for the better, assuming we take our medicine.

Let us now look at the following additional scriptures:

God Requests Us to Not Provoke Him	
Proverbs 14:31 *He who oppresses the poor taunts his Maker, But he who is gracious to the needy honors Him.*	Proverbs 17:5 *He who mocks the poor taunts his Maker; He who rejoices at calamity will not go unpunished.*

Examples of Being Provoked and Handling it Well	
Psalm 106:28-31 They joined themselves also to Baal-peor, And ate sacrifices offered to the dead. Thus they provoked Him to anger with their deeds, And the plague broke out among them. Then Phinehas stood up and interposed, And so the plague was stayed. And it was reckoned to him for righteousness, To all generations forever.	*Job 2:6-10 So the LORD said to Satan, "Behold, he is in your power, only spare his life." Then Satan went out from the presence of the LORD and smote Job with sore boils from the sole of his foot to the crown of his head. And he took a potsherd to scrape himself while he was sitting among the ashes. Then his wife said to him, "Do you still hold fast your integrity? Curse God and die!" But he said to her, "You speak as one of the foolish women speaks. Shall we indeed accept good from God and not accept adversity?" In all this Job did not sin with his lips.*
2 Samuel 16:5-6 and 9-12 *When King David came to Bahurim, behold, there came out from there a man of the family of the house of Saul whose name was Shimei, the son of Gera; he came out cursing continually as he came. He threw stones at David and at all the servants of King David; and all the people and all the mighty men were at his right hand and at his left. Then Abishai the son of Zeruiah said to the king, "Why should this dead dog curse my lord the king? Let me go over now and cut off his head." But the king said, "What have I to do with you, O sons of Zeruiah? If he curses, and if the LORD has told him, 'Curse David,' then who shall say, 'Why have you done so?' " Then David said to Abishai and to all his servants, "Behold, my son who came out from me seeks my life; how much more now this Benjamite? Let him alone and let him curse, for the LORD has told him. "Perhaps the LORD will look on my affliction and return good to me instead of his cursing this day."*	

Deuteronomy 9:16-21 *And I saw that you had indeed sinned against the LORD your God. You had made for yourselves a molten calf; you had turned aside quickly from the way which the LORD had commanded you. I took hold of the two tablets and threw them from my hands and smashed them before your eyes. I fell down before the LORD, as at the first, forty days and nights; I neither ate bread nor drank water, because of all your sin which you had committed in doing what was evil in the sight of the LORD to provoke Him to anger. For I was afraid of the anger and hot displeasure with which the LORD was wrathful against you in order to destroy you, but the LORD listened to me that time also. The LORD was angry enough with Aaron to destroy him; so I also prayed for Aaron at the same time. I took your sinful thing, the calf which you had made, and burned it with fire and crushed it, grinding it very small until it was as fine as dust; and I threw its dust into the brook that came down from the mountain.*

Examples of Being Provoked and Handling it Poorly
Psalm 106:32-33 *They also provoked Him to wrath at the waters of Meribah, So that it went hard with Moses on their account; Because they were rebellious against His Spirit, He spoke rashly with his lips.*

Perhaps these final words will also inspire us to maintain our cool when we are provoked.

Quotes

The neat middle-aged executive peers out from the television screen. "Hello," he says, his face crinkling into a sheepish grin. "I'm from General Telephone." Boos and hisses explode off-camera. "Now, I'm aware that General Telephone provides less than adequate service." Plop. A rotten tomato slides down his chin. "But we're spending $200 million in California this year on improving our service." He is hit with an egg. "Cables, switches, personnel, everything." A cream pie splatters over his face. "Thank you for your patience," he mumbles through the goo.

In another commercial, a woman at a crowded cocktail party asks her husband to say something funny. "General Telephone," he replies, and everyone *falls into paroxysms of laughter. The punch line: "We know some people think our service is laughable, but we're spending $200 million in California this year to improve it. What's so funny about that?"*

These vignettes have appeared on Los Angeles television as part of a zany General Telephone of California. By tacitly conceding the company's mistakes, the admen hope that the campaign will win sympathy and understanding among the system's many disgruntled users.

John Wesley tells of a man whom year after year he thought of contemptuously as covetous. One day when he contributed to one of Wesley's charities a gift that seemed very small, Wesley's indignation knew no bounds, and he raked him fore and aft with blistering condemnation.

Wesley tells in his diary that the man quietly said: "I know a man who at each week's beginning goes to market and buys a penny's worth of parsnips and takes them home to boil in water, and all that week he has parsnips for his food and water for his drink; and food and drink alike cost him a penny a week." The man had been skimping in order to pay off debts contracted before his conversion. —Christ's Ambassadors Herald

Several years ago a Santa Fe train was speeding through Oklahoma. In one of the coaches sat a young woman desperately trying to take care of a restless baby, whose crying was evidently annoying some of the passengers.

Across the aisle sat a stout fellow, a picture of comfort and rich living. He glowered over at the woman and shouted: "Can't you keep that child quiet?" On taking a further look at the young lady, he noticed that her dress was one of mourning.

Then he heard her say gently: "I cannot help it. The child is not mine. I am doing my best."

"Where is its mother?" asked the portly passenger.

"In her coffin, sir," answered the young lady, "in the baggage car up ahead."

The steely eyes of the fat fellow filled with tears. He got up, took the babe in his arms, kissed it, and then walked up and down the aisle with the child, trying his best to soothe the motherless little one and make up for his harshness. —Selected

XOgesis

Ned: "KJ in trouble again?"

KJ: "My sister keeps saying that I am provoking her, but I don't know what she is talking about and I don't even know what that means."

Ned: "Why don't you just turn the other cheek?"

KJ: "No thanks. That will really make her mad."

Ned: "Huh?!"

KJ: "I was just very innocently painting a little sign when she was sleeping..."

Ned: "So you weren't bothering her?"

KJ: "I was very careful while I was painting on her face and it was going to look really cool and I was only half finished when she just woke up and yelled at me. So you see doing the other cheek would not really be a good idea here..."

From KJ & Friends ™ © 2010 by G Doulos

OLD TESTAMENT EXAMPLES [Deut 9] [Isaiah 65]

Describe how the LORD handles being ***Provoked*** or prevents us from acting poorly after being ***Provoked,*** in these passages.

Describe how the LORD has been nice to you even after He has been ***Provoked*** by you or by someone you know.

List a way you will handle being ***Provoked*** this week. Prepare a concise teaching on combating being ***Provoked***.

My Lesson Plan

Extra Credit – Pick any of the 10 commandments and think about how not losing control after being ***Provoked*** will help you fulfill the commandment.

CHARACTERISTIC OF LOVE

Discussion

The word used in the Greek here for *take into account*, λογίζεται (*logizetai*), basically means *to keep a record of events or actions for the sake of some future purpose*. A secular use of this word would be *to reckon* or *charge*. Reckoning has to do with settling accounts and has to do with calculations. We can reconcile a bank account by making sure we have meticulously accounted for all expenses and deposits. We can reckon the height of a building by estimating how many floors it contains. We can reckon one's exact age by counting the days since their birth date. Reckon also has the idea of thoughtful musings as in, "I reckon I have been fortunate to work at a job I love." And of course we all know about the *Day of Reckoning*, where we give an accounting of our actions to God. So this word is innocent enough in its uses unless it is used for hurtful purposes.

Let us look at the rest of the verse. Now while the NASB mentions that love does not take into account *a wrong suffered*, the Greek for *a wrong suffered*, is simply, τὸ κακόν (*to kakon*), *the bad*. We can translate this aspect of love succinctly as *love does not record bad*.

In today's modern society we are very familiar with recording things. Cameras which take still pictures have been around for a long time. Nowadays there are video recorders, voice recorders, music recorders, analog, digital — you name it.

Even cell phones now can record voice, as well as take still pictures and videos. Most of us are familiar with recording our favorite TV shows and movies. In our digital world it is easy to record and store information on our computer's hard drive or on a small digital media card or thumb drive. Those Old Testament scribes would be so jealous (in a good way).

But in the realm of love with regard to recording and remembering other people's sins and faults we are told to not hit the record button. The human brain has a tremendous capacity for remembering things and although we are not in the same league as a computer, our total memory capacity and processing speed is none too shabby. Plus, we have several advantages over computers. We do not need a new operating system or hard drive every three or four years, and our hard drive (actually the brain is kind of soft) lasts for up to one hundred years. We do not need a power supply, and with a little work we can have instant recall of our favorite information.

In an article by Ralph C. Merkle, first appearing in *Foresight Update No. 4*, in October 1988, he details an experiment involving human memory capability. The remarkable result of this work was that human beings remembered very nearly two bits per second under all the experimental conditions. The type of learning: visual, verbal, musical, or whatever did not seem to matter. That corresponds to about fifteen bytes per minute, and about one kilobyte per hour.

One kilobyte of information for example would be the text of the first seven verses of 1 Corinthians chapter thirteen (our study chapter). Thus if we carefully reviewed these verses for about one hour they would be initially committed to memory, and subsequent review sessions would keep them in our memory.

Well that is quite nice. So now we have instant recall of our favorite scripture verses. And if we dwell on them over the next months and years they will always be with us in an instant to refresh our heart, soul, mind and strength. But what happens when we dwell on the wrong type of information?

Unfortunately when we put to memory the sins of others and we dwell on these unforgiven injustices, they are committed to memory also and are instantly available. How easily we can see this. These memorized transgressions, these fault accounts, are recited word for word when we become upset with a person that may have the misfortune to have a sin account with us.

It is unfair to this person to recite his or her past faults, and unhealthy and sinful for us to do so. A legal term related to this is called *double jeopardy,* and can be defined as a procedural defense that forbids a defendant from being tried twice for the same crime on the same set of facts. In many countries the guarantee against being twice put in jeopardy is a constitutional right.

So how can we forgive and forget? The key is not recording, not reciting, not dwelling on the sins of others. The less we dwell on the sins of others, the more those old memories will eventually fall out of our memory. Another way to remove imbedded sin accounts from our brains is to replace them with accounts full of good thoughts. To use computer terminology, these new good accounts will be copied over the sin accounts and thus will replace them and remove them from our brain into the trash can. This is very biblical as Philippians 4:8 states,

Finally, brethren, whatever is true, whatever is honorable, whatever is right, whatever is pure, whatever is lovely, whatever is of good repute, if there is any excellence and if anything worthy of praise, dwell on these things.

Keeping account of the sins of others is preventing something really important from happening. What is that? It is preventing the ministry of reconciliation. How important is reconciliation? Read the following:

2 Corinthians 5:16–19 *Therefore from now on we recognize no one according to the flesh; even though we have known Christ according to the flesh, yet now we know Him in this way no longer. Therefore if anyone is in Christ, he is a new creature; the old things passed away; behold, new things have come. Now all these things are from God, who reconciled us to Himself through Christ and gave us the ministry of reconciliation,*

namely, that God was in Christ reconciling the world to Himself, not counting their trespasses against them, and He has committed to us the word of reconciliation.

Wow! We are actually ministers of reconciliation. However, we cannot be involved with the ministry of reconciliation if we are counting, recording, reciting and holding transgressions against others. Our ministry will fail miserably. It is hoped this helps clean up some troublesome relationships. Remember each day we need to wipe everyone's slate clean. We can be thankful that God does this for us! Think good thoughts and do not record the bad.

Remember the goal — reconciliation. Our constant mentioning of people's failings (even if it is not to their face) is just what the devil does. Satan is the accuser of the brethren. So repeating someone else's sin is doing Satan's job for him. It is not that we should never share with others how we have been treated. After we share our story, however, perhaps we should also mention that we have forgiven the person. If we cannot bring ourselves to forgive someone completely just yet, we need to be very careful to control our tongue. We do not want to turn into a bitter person who is constantly holding grudges against others.

Proverbs 17:9 *He who conceals a transgression seeks love, But he who repeats a matter separates intimate friends.*

If we are having trouble letting go of the past sins of others, try these symbolic (albeit simplistic) actions. We can try putting down all the faults of the person we are constantly upset with on a board or piece of paper. Then we pray and once and for all truly forgive that person as we wipe the board clean, or we can burn the paper, removing their faults from our memory for all time. Our God will surely give us the strength to do this! His mercies towards us are new every morning, and He can give us the ability to extend those same tender mercies through forgiveness to others we know. What a burden will be removed. We will be as light as a feather. Praise God! Besides, we have more important and exciting things to keep in our memory as we embark on our ministry of reconciliation!

Let us now look at the following additional scriptures:

God's View of Reconciliation	
Jeremiah 18:8 *if that nation against which I have spoken turns from its evil, I will relent concerning the calamity I planned to bring on it.*	Matthew 18:21–22 *Then Peter came and said to Him, "Lord, how often shall my brother sin against me and I forgive him? Up to seven times?" Jesus said to him, "I do not say to you, up to seven times, but up to seventy times seven.*
Psalm 32:1–2 *How blessed is he whose transgression is forgiven, Whose sin is covered! How blessed is the man to whom the LORD does not impute iniquity, And in whose spirit there is no deceit!*	Romans 4:8 *Blessed is the man whose sin the Lord will not take into account.*

Examples of Reconciliation
Luke 15:11-24 *And He said, "A man had two sons. The younger of them said to his father, 'Father, give me the share of the estate that falls to me.' So he divided his wealth between them. And not many days later, the younger son gathered everything together and went on a journey into a distant country, and there he squandered his estate with loose living. Now when he had spent everything, a severe famine occurred in that country, and he began to be impoverished. So he went and hired himself out to one of the citizens of that country, and he sent him into his fields to feed swine. And he would have gladly filled his stomach with the pods that the swine were eating, and no one was giving anything to him. But when he came to his senses, he said, 'How many of my father's hired men have more than enough bread, but I am dying here with hunger!' I will get up and go to my father, and will say to him, 'Father, I have sinned against heaven, and in your sight; I am no longer worthy to be called your son; make me as one of your hired men.' So he got up and came to his father. But while he was still a long way off, his father saw him and felt compassion for him, and ran and embraced him and kissed him. And the son said to him, 'Father, I have sinned against heaven and in your sight; I am no longer worthy to be called your son.' But the father said to his slaves, 'Quickly bring out the best robe and put it on him, and put a ring on his hand and sandals on his feet; and bring the fattened calf, kill it, and let us eat and celebrate; for this son of mine was dead and has come to life again; he was lost and has been found.' And they began to celebrate."*

Examples of Reconciliation
Genesis 50:15–21 *When Joseph's brothers saw that their father was dead, they said, "What if Joseph bears a grudge against us and pays us back in full for all the wrong which we did to him!" So they sent a message to Joseph, saying, "Your father charged before he died, saying, 'Thus you shall say to Joseph, Please forgive, I beg you, the transgression of your brothers and their sin, for they did you wrong.' And now, please forgive the transgression of the servants of the God of your father." And Joseph wept when they spoke to him. Then his brothers also came and fell down before him and said, "Behold, we are your servants." But Joseph said to them, "Do not be afraid, for am I in God's place? As for you, you meant evil against me, but God meant it for good in order to bring about this present result, to preserve many people alive. So therefore, do not be afraid; I will provide for you and your little ones." So he comforted them and spoke kindly to them.*

Examples of Taking into Account a Wrong Suffered	
Genesis 27:41 *So Esau bore a grudge against Jacob because of the blessing with which his father had blessed him; and Esau said to himself, "The days of mourning for my father are near; then I will kill my brother Jacob."*	Esther 3:5–6 *When Haman saw that Mordecai neither bowed down nor paid homage to him, Haman was filled with rage. But he disdained to lay hands on Mordecai alone, for they had told him who the people of Mordecai were; therefore Haman sought to destroy all the Jews, the people of Mordecai, who were throughout the whole kingdom of Ahasuerus.*
Acts 15:36–39 *After some days Paul said to Barnabas, "Let us return and visit the brethren in every city in which we proclaimed the word of the Lord, and see how they are." Barnabas wanted to take John, called Mark, along with them also. But Paul kept insisting that they should not take him along who had deserted them in Pamphylia and had not gone with them to the work. And there occurred such a sharp disagreement that they separated from one another, and Barnabas took Mark with him and sailed away to Cyprus.*	

Perhaps these final words will also inspire us to not keep accounts of the faults and sins of others, and treat each other with a clean slate each day.

Quotes

David H. Fink, author of Release From Nervous Tension, wrote an article for the Coronet Magazine, in which he made a striking suggestion as to how we can overcome mental and emotional tensions.

As a psychiatrist for the Veterans Administration he was familiar with 10,000 case histories in this field. Thousands of people, who were mentally and emotionally "tied up," had asked Dr. Fink for some short, magic-button cure for nervousness. In his search for such a cure he studied two groups; the first group was made up of thousands of people who were suffering from mental and emotional disturbances; the second group contained only those, thousands of them, who were free from such tensions.

Gradually one fact began to stand out: those who suffered from extreme tension had one trait in common—they were habitual faultfinders, constant critics of people and things around them, whereas the men and women who were free of all tensions were the least faultfinding. It would seem that the habit of criticizing is a prelude or mark of the nervous and of the mentally unbalanced.

A preacher had on his desk a special book labeled "Complaints of members against one another." When one of his people called to tell him the faults of another he would say, "Well, here's my complaint book. I'll write down what you say, and you can sign it. Then when I have to take up the matter officially I shall know what I may expect you to testify to." The sight of the open book and the ready pen had its effect, "Oh, no, I couldn't sign anything like that!" and no entry was made. The preacher said he kept the book for forty years, opened it probably a thousand times, and never wrote a line in it.

This story was told of General Robert E. Lee: Hearing General Lee speak in the highest terms to President Davis about a certain officer, another officer, greatly astonished, said to him, "General, do you know that the man of whom you speak so highly to the President is one of your bitterest enemies, and misses no opportunity to malign you?" "Yes," replied General Lee, "but the President asked my opinion of him; he did not ask for his opinion of me."
– Sunshine Magazine

I will speak ill of no man, not even in the matter of truth, but rather excuse the faults I hear, and, upon proper occasions, speak all the good I know of everybody. —Benjamin Franklin

King Henry VI of England had it said of him: "He never forgot anything but injuries." Of Cranmer it was said: "If you want to get a favor from him, do him a wrong." Emerson said of Lincoln: "His heart was as great as the world, but there was no room in it for the memory of a wrong." Spurgeon gives this advice: "Cultivate forbearance till your heart yields a fine crop of it. Pray for a short memory as to unkindness." —Rev. David L. Currens

XOgesis

Naz: "KJ, why are you erasing those check marks on your white board?"

KJ: "I was keeping a record of every time this kid Richard did something bad to me."

Naz: "Why don't you just forgive him like the Bible says?"

KJ: "I did, but I didn't want to forget how many times he's been mean to me."

Naz: "Don't you know forgetting the wrongs people do to you is part of forgiveness? If you don't forget the past wrongs, then when that same person wrongs you, you will be upset for that and everything else he has ever done to you. That weight of sin will drag you down. And you will be punishing people over and over again for something that they thought was forgiven..."

KJ: "Well, that is why I am erasing these marks and because ..."

Naz: "Well now that is very nice of you... hey, is that a black eye ???"

KJ: "Yup. Richard found out about my check marks and he told me I didn't need them 'cause he would give me something to remember his faults better."

OLD TESTAMENT EXAMPLES [Neh 9:1-31] [Jer 31:31-34] [Isa 6:1-8]

Describe how the LORD ***Seeks Reconciliation*** in these passages.

Describe how the LORD has been ***Reconciling*** you or someone that you know.

List a way you will ***Not Record the Bad*** this week. Prepare a concise teaching on ***Reconciliation***.

My Application:

My Lesson Plan

Extra Credit – Pick any of the 10 commandments and think about how not ***Taking into Account a Wrong Suffered*** will help you fulfill the commandment.

CHARACTERISTIC OF LOVE

Discussion

The phrase used in the Greek here for *does not rejoice in unrighteousness*, οὐ χαίρει ἐπὶ τῇ ἀδικίᾳ (*ou chairei epi tē adikia*) translated word for word would be: *not it rejoices in the unrighteousness*. Before we tackle the implications behind the word *unrighteousness* let us delve into this simple word *rejoice*.

The noun forms related to the verb would include χαρά (*chara*) and χάρις (*charis*), joy and grace. Joy is more than happiness as it is more independent of happenings. It is more of a state of mind or being although it may ebb and flow. The verb form of grace includes the idea of bestowing favor and blessing. Rejoice is also used as a greeting. So if someone comes to our door we can say *Rejoice*, meaning *hey good to see you, come right in, we welcome you with favor and blessing*! We are commanded to rejoice in the Lord and the idea is that we should embrace Him spiritually and bestow favor and blessing on Him. Also, what we consider a blessing is what brings us joy.

What brings out the joy in us, what we welcome with open arms into our lives, what we bless and bestow favor upon is very important. It can define who we are. It can show us how we have defined our priorities in life. Again, we hate to beat a dead horse but this word, like jealousy and zealousness, can be good for us or bad for us depending on what we decide to embrace. The joy of the Lord can be our strength, but the joy derived by embracing the world can lead to big trouble.

So what does the Bible tell us concerning unrighteousness? Why should we not bestow favor on and embrace unrighteousness? In the New Testament a person who embraces unrighteousness is termed *unrighteous*. We can see how the Bible contrasts a person who rejoices in unrighteousness versus a person who does not in the following verses.

Matthew 5:45: *so that you may be sons of your Father who is in heaven; for He causes His sun to rise on the evil and the good, and sends rain on the righteous and the unrighteous.*

1 Corinthians 6:1 *Does any one of you, when he has a case against his neighbor, dare to go to law before the unrighteous and not before the saints?*

1 Corinthians 6:9–10 *Or do you not know that the unrighteous will not inherit the kingdom of God? Do not be deceived; neither fornicators, nor idolaters, nor adulterers, nor effeminate, nor homosexuals, nor thieves, nor the covetous, nor drunkards, nor revilers, nor swindlers, will inherit the kingdom of God.*

Based on these and other verses we can put together a table of attributes that describes the righteous versus the unrighteous.

Unrighteous		**Righteous**
Evil		Good
Fornicators	Idolaters	Saints
Adulterers	Effeminate	Just
Homosexuals	Thieves	Godly
Covetous	Drunkards	Faithful
Revilers	Swindlers	True
Unjust		

From the previous table we can clearly see the distinction between what is righteous and what is not righteous. For now we will skip the theological discussion of righteousness as it pertains to right standing with God. For now we need to grasp what we should not rejoice in.

Another facet we need to mention is that it is possible to rejoice in something without outwardly identifying with it. We will discuss this even more fully when we discuss the next portion of our study verse (1 Corinthians 13:6). While we may not overtly or consistently behave in the manner of the unrighteous, we may also not be upset about the behavior either. We need to be careful about the books we read and the shows we watch. In some cases, most likely our weak areas, we may secretly rejoice in the bad behavior as well. Our attitude about certain behavior is important because it can lead to action. We may think to ourselves that we do not always participate in a certain behavior, but if we still see nothing really wrong with it, we may find that we are soon becoming a frequent flyer. We may not outwardly associate ourselves with people who are unrighteous, but inwardly we may embrace some of their sinful attributes. We need to catch ourselves before this becomes a habit. Otherwise the Lord may have to use discipline in order to modify our behavior or attitude. We need to be pure in heart and not compromise God's moral code of righteousness.

Let us now look at the following additional scriptures:

God's View of Unrighteousness	
2 Samuel 7:14 *I will be a father to him and he will be a son to Me; when he commits iniquity, I will correct him with the rod of men and the strokes of the sons of men,*	2 Chronicles 19:7 *Now then let the fear of the LORD be upon you; be very careful what you do, for the LORD our God will have no part in unrighteousness or partiality or the taking of a bribe.*
Psalm 66:18 *If I regard wickedness in my heart, The Lord will not hear;*	Psalm 92:15 *To declare that the LORD is upright; He is my rock, and there is no unrighteousness in Him.*

Examples of Unrighteous Behavior	
Psalm 52:2 *Your tongue devises destruction, Like a sharp razor, O worker of deceit.*	Lamentations 2:14 *Your prophets have seen for you False and foolish visions; And they have not exposed your iniquity So as to restore you from captivity, But they have seen for you false and misleading oracles.*
Ezekiel 12:2 *Son of man, you live in the midst of the rebellious house, who have eyes to see but do not see, ears to hear but do not hear; for they are a rebellious house.*	

Examples of Not Rejoicing in Unrighteousness	
Psalm 17:3 *You have tried my heart; You have visited me by night; You have tested me and You find nothing; I have purposed that my mouth will not transgress.*	Psalm 119:29 *Remove the false way from me, And graciously grant me Your law.*
Proverbs 11:5 *The righteousness of the blameless will smooth his way, But the wicked will fall by his own wickedness.*	

Perhaps these final words will also inspire us to avoid rejoicing in unrighteousness.

Quotes

Billy Sunday, the baseball evangelist and reformer, never spared himself nor those he wanted to help in the vigor of his attacks on sin. He thundered against evil from the Gay Nineties through the Great Depression. He preached Christ as the only answer to man's needs until his death in 1935.

"I'm against sin," he said. "I'll kick it as long as I've got a foot, and I'll fight it as long as I've got a fist. I'll butt it as long as I've got a head. I'll bite it as long as I've got a tooth. When I'm old and fistless and footless and toothless, I'll gum it till I go home to Glory and it goes home to perdition."

A flippant youth asked a preacher, "You say that unsaved people carry a weight of sin. I feel nothing. How heavy is sin? Is it ten pounds? Eighty pounds?" The preacher replied by asking the youth, "If you laid a four-hundred-pound weight on a corpse, would it feel the load?" The youth replied, "It would feel nothing, because it is dead." The preacher concluded, "That spirit, too, is indeed dead which feels no load of sin or is indifferent to its burden and flippant about its presence." The youth was silenced!

- *We sing "Sweet Hour of Prayer" and are content with 5–10 minutes a day.*
- *We sing "Onward Christian Soldiers" and wait to be drafted into His service.*
- *We sing "O for a Thousand Tongues to Sing" and don't use the one we have.*
- *We sing "There Shall be Showers of Blessing" but do not come when it rains.*
- *We sing "Blest Be the Tie That Binds" and let the least little offense sever it.*
- *We sing "Serve the Lord With Gladness" and gripe about all we have to do.*
- *We sing "I Love to Tell the Story" and never mention it at all.*
- *We sing "We're Marching to Zion" but fail to march to worship or church school.*
- *We sing "Cast Thy Burden on the Lord" and worry ourselves into a nervous breakdown.*
- *We sing "The Whole Wide World for Jesus" and never invite our next-door neighbor.*
- *We sing "O Day of Rest and Gladness" and wear ourselves out traveling, cutting grass or playing golf on Sunday.*
- *We sing "Throw Out the Lifeline" and content ourselves with throwing out a fishing line.*

XOgesis

Naz: "KJ, you are all dressed up. Who are you pretending to be?"

KJ: "I am Zack Powers international hunter of evil."

Naz: "Zack Powers. He does some really bad stuff too."

KJ: "Yeah, but all the good he does is more than the bad."

Naz: "You should be careful not to idolize someone like that because you are promoting the bad as well as the good."

KJ: "But the good is gooder than the bad."

Naz: "You can never do enough good so that your bad is excused."

KJ: "Even if I catch a million bad guys and maybe just cheat on one test question at school, the bad isn't wiped out?"

Naz: "Nope."

KJ: "What if I rescue a billion people from being captured by bad guys and just say a few bad words???"

Naz: "Nope."

KJ: "What good is it being an international hunter of evil if you don't get any breaks?"

From KJ & Friends ™ © 2010 by G Doulos

OLD TESTAMENT EXAMPLES [2 Chron 19:1-7] [Mal 2:1-9]

Describe how the LORD does not ***Rejoice in Unrighteousness*** or prevents us from doing so in these passages.

Describe how the LORD has been asking you to not ***Rejoice In Unrighteousness*** and/or someone that you know.

List a way you will not ***Rejoice in Unrighteousness*** this week. Prepare a concise teaching on combating ***Rejoicing in Unrighteousness.***

My Application:

My Lesson Plan

Extra Credit – Pick any of the 10 commandments and think about how not ***Rejoicing in Unrighteousness*** will help you fulfill the commandment.

CHARACTERISTIC OF LOVE

Rejoices with the Truth

Discussion

The phrase used in the Greek here for *rejoices with the truth*, συνχαίρει δὲ τῇ ἀληθείᾳ (*sunchairei de tē alētheia*) basically means *but it rejoices with the truth.* In addition or perhaps even more emphatically, this phrase means *to become associated with and identified in connection with the truth.* If we look at the whole of verse six together we may ask ourselves why the verse did not say *love does not rejoice in unrighteousness, but rejoices in righteousness.* Let us look at the very subtle yet challenging reason why the verse is framed as it is.

First we can look at the first part of the verse and ask ourselves a few questions. Is it easier to say we do not approve of any unrighteousness, or is it easier to say that we will never be part of an evil gang? Well, for most of us it is easier to say we will not be part (action) of a gang of evildoers, than it is to say that we will go on record as saying we despise (attitude) all unrighteousness.

Jesus alluded to this when He talked about committing adultery in our heart. It may be easy for some people to say, "Oh no I have never committed adultery" (action). However, have they actually committed adultery in their heart (attitude)? In a similar passage, Jesus says one may say that he has never actually killed someone, but perhaps in his mind, he has called the person very vile names and wished for his death. So He forbids killing people, the outward action, but also forbids rejoicing inwardly in the unrighteous thoughts of slander and wishing harm on others. This underlines the message in our previously studied characteristic that states *Loves does not rejoice in unrighteousness.*

But to go on the holy offensive we must not limit ourselves in saying that we believe in the Ten Commandments and in being good. That would be just rejoicing *in* righteousness. We must identify ourselves with these beliefs by actively living them out and taking a stand for them even if it is unpopular. We need to be a person of integrity, of honor, and leave cowardly ways behind. We must *rejoice with the truth*. To follow this exhortation we must do more than just meekly identify ourselves with truth. We must completely embrace the truth, including rejoicing at the thought of being persecuted for the truth. When we think of what brings us joy in the Christian life, one of those things should be associating with and identifying with the truth. Joy is also a fruit of the Spirit. The following statements taken from various passages in the Bible will illustrate other sources of joy for the believer.

- When we are persecuted because our reward is great in heaven
- In affliction
- When demons are subjugated
- When a sinner repents
- When miracles are seen
- Upon hearing and following God's commandments
- In seeing Jesus risen from the dead
- When the Kingdom of God is described as *righteousness and peace and joy in the Holy Spirit*
- The people we disciple
- Discipline
- Standing firm
- Festivals
- Taking refuge in God
- God's presence
- Singing, shouting, and playing songs
- Being a counselor of peace

Let us now look at the following additional scriptures:

God's View of Rejoicing with the Truth	
Joshua 24:14 *Now, therefore, fear the* LORD *and serve Him in sincerity and truth; and put away the gods which your fathers served beyond the River and in Egypt, and serve the* LORD.	1 Samuel 12:24 *Only fear the Lord and serve Him in truth with all your heart; for consider what great things He has done for you.*
Psalm 51:6 *Behold, You desire truth in the innermost being, And in the hidden part You will make me know wisdom.*	

Examples of Rejoicing with the Truth	
Psalm 40:10 *I have not hidden Your righteousness within my heart; I have spoken of Your faithfulness and Your salvation; I have not concealed Your lovingkindness and Your truth from the great congregation.*	John 17:17–19 *Sanctify them in the truth; Your word is truth. As You sent Me into the world, I also have sent them into the world. For their sakes I sanctify Myself, that they themselves also may be sanctified in truth.*

Examples of Not Rejoicing with the Truth	
Acts 5:1–3 *But a man named Ananias, with his wife Sapphira, sold a piece of property, and kept back some of the price for himself, with his wife's full knowledge, and bringing a portion of it, he laid it at the apostles' feet. But Peter said, "Ananias, why has Satan filled your heart to lie to the Holy Spirit and to keep back some of the price of the land?*	Isaiah 48:1 *Hear this, O house of Jacob, who are named Israel And who came forth from the loins of Judah, Who swear by the name of the* LORD *And invoke the God of Israel, But not in truth nor in righteousness.*
Galatians 2:14 *But when I saw that they were not straightforward about the truth of the gospel, I said to Cephas in the presence of all, "If you, being a Jew, live like the Gentiles and not like the Jews, how is it that you compel the Gentiles to live like Jews?"*	

Perhaps these final words will also inspire us to rejoice with the truth.

Quotes

It is said that when Grover Cleveland was a boy he insisted upon returning the egg that a neighbor's hen daily laid on the Cleveland side of the fence. Thus he early began to give proof of the honesty that marked him as a man and a future President of the United States. Faithfulness to high principles in such little things leads to honesty in matters of greater importance.

When he was 24 years old, Abraham Lincoln served as the postmaster of New Salem, Illinois, for which he was paid an annual salary of $55.70. Even then, 24 years before he entered the White House, the rail-splitter was showing the character that earned him the title of "Honest Abe." The New Salem post office was closed in 1836, but it was several years before an agent arrived from Washington to settle accounts with ex-postmaster Lincoln, who was a struggling lawyer not doing too well. The agent informed him that there was $17 due the government. Lincoln crossed the room, opened an old trunk and took out a yellowed cotton rag bound with string. Untying it, he spread out the cloth and there was the $17. He had been holding it untouched for all the years. "I never use any man's money but my own," he said.

When the father of the great Emmanuel Kant was an old man he made a perilous journey through the forests of Poland to his native country of Silesia. On the way he encountered a band of robbers who demanded all his valuables, finally asking: "Have you given us all?" and only letting him go when he answered, "All." When safely out of their sight his hand touched something hard in the hem of his robe. It was his gold, sewn there for safety and quite forgotten by him in his fear and confusion.

At once he hurried back to find the robbers, and having found them, he said meekly: "I have told you what was not true; it was unintentional. I was too terrified to think. Here, take the gold in my robes." Then to the old man's astonishment nobody offered to take his gold. Presently one went and brought back his purse. Another restored his book of prayer, while still another led his horse toward him and helped him to mount. They then unitedly entreated his blessing, and watched him slowly ride away. Goodness had triumphed over evil. – J.A. Clark

An American vessel named Nancy, suspected of carrying contraband, was seized by a British revenue cutter in 1799 and taken into Port Royal. Before it was boarded, however, the crew disposed of the forbidden part of the cargo and the captain likewise threw overboard the ship's papers, substituting a faked set he had prepared for such an emergency.

At the trial he and the officers were about to be acquitted of the charge of smuggling, for lack of evidence, when the master of another cutter walked into the court with the Nancy's original papers. His men had discovered them in the stomach of a shark they had harpooned that morning. Consequently, the defendants were convicted.

Today, these documents, called "The Shark's Papers," are on exhibition in the Institute of Jamaica in Kingston, and the shark's head is preserved in the Royal United Service Institution in London. —Selected

In my youth, science was more important to me than either man or God. I worshipped science. Its advance had surpassed man's wildest dreams. It took many years for me to discover that science, with all its brilliance, lights only a middle chapter of creation.

I saw the aircraft I love destroying the civilization I expected it to save. Now I understand that spiritual truth is more essential to a nation than the mortar in its cities' walls. For when the actions of a people are undergirded by spiritual truths, there is safety. When spiritual truths are rejected, it is only a matter of time before civilization will collapse.

We must understand spiritual truths and apply them to our modern life. We must draw strength from the almost forgotten virtues of simplicity, humility, contemplation and prayer. It requires a dedication beyond science, beyond self, but the rewards are great and it is our only hope. —Charles Lindbergh

Few international celebrities have been so baffling as Charles Lindbergh. It was unreasonable to many—yet remarkable to others—why he did not capitalize more on his flight across the Atlantic in 1927. But commercializing the flight was the last thing he wanted. One friend estimated that Lindbergh could have made five million dollars in one week if he would have accepted the hundreds of offers to sign testimonials, write books, or go into the movies.

William Randolph Hearst offered Lindbergh five hundred thousand dollars if he would star in a film about aviation. He declined a vaudeville contract to which was attached a one-million- dollar guarantee. A movie company made him another million-dollar offer; it was turned down. Another movie company upped its offer to five million. Money came to him as gifts, but it was always returned. An associate summed it up: "Lindbergh won't take money he hasn't earned."

When the citizens of High Wycombe, England, elect a new mayor, all the town councilors are weighed in public, following an ancient custom. Those whose weight is less than or at least not more than when they took office are warmly applauded—they have not grown fat at public expense. —Ospitalita Albergh

Once when the famous Bishop Warren A. Candler was preaching to a large audience, he used as his text the story of Ananias and Sapphira, who told a lie to God and were struck dead. The old bishop roared: "God doesn't strike people dead for lying like He used to. If He did, where would I be?" When his audience snickered a bit, he roared back, "I tell you where I would be. I would be right here preaching to an empty house!"—Optimist Magazine

XOgesis

Ned: "KJ, you are back from your soccer tournament?"

KJ: "Yep, we got 2nd place, but we did win the sportsmanship award."

Ned: "Well that's great because that's the best award. Your zeal for what is honest and true is more important than winning or losing a game."

KJ: "Yeah, that's what coach said, but I would rather get the 1st place trophy."

Ned: "That's not a good attitude. What if your whole team thought that, then how..."

KJ: "Everyone on the team does think that."

Ned: "Then how did your team win the sportsmanship award?"

KJ: "Because we were the only team that shook the hands with the players and referees after every game."

Ned: "Well, at least that is something."

KJ: "Yeah, if we didn't, coach said we'd be running sprints for the next ten practices."

Ned: "So you won the sportsmanship award because you were threatened with punishment?"

KJ: "You mean there are actually people out there that want to be good sports without getting rewards or fearing punishments?"

OLD TESTAMENT EXAMPLES [Exodus 18:21-23] [Malachi 4]

Describe how the LORD ***Rejoices with the Truth*** or prevents us from not ***Rejoicing with the Truth,*** in these passages.

Describe how the LORD has been teaching you or someone you know to ***Rejoice with the Truth.***

List a way you will ***Rejoice with the Truth*** this week. Prepare a concise teaching on how to ***Rejoice with the Truth.***

My Application:

My Lesson Plan

Extra Credit – Pick any of the 10 commandments and think about how ***Rejoicing with the Truth*** will help you fulfill the commandment.

CHARACTERISTIC OF LOVE

Bears

Discussion

The word used in the Greek here for *bears*, στέγει (*stegei*), comes from a stem meaning *to cover, to conceal.* It is a relatively rare term but exists in both Greek prose and common speech. Its basic meaning is *to keep covered*, but this gives it such senses as *to protect, to ward off, to hold back, to resist*, to *support*, to be *watertight*, to *bear*, and to *sustain.* It can also mean *to keep secret, to keep silent*, and *to keep a confidence.* The noun form literally means *a roof.* The meaning, then, is perhaps that love *covers* all things. The NIV translates this word as *protects.* This love keeps silent about unfavorable matters while it withstands the storms that rage on the outside. And yet the soul is quieted and is kept safe under the roof of this love that is bearing up under all things.

What may be the motivation for this all-bearing love? Let us look at another verse from Corinthians.

1 Corinthians 9:12 *If others share the right over you, do we not more? Nevertheless, we did not use this right, but we endure all things so that we will cause no hindrance to the gospel of Christ.*

In this case the reason this love is bearing all things is so that the Gospel of Christ would be spread without any hindrances. It is important that we bear up under all things for the right reasons and motivation. Parents who work hard and bear many hardships for the sake of meeting their children's needs (not necessarily all their wants) are good examples of bearing all things. Another good example would be a Christian bearing up under ridicule and prejudice, not becoming angry or seeking revenge, when verbally attacked just for taking a stand for the truth. Bearing unlawful or vicious physical abuse is a different story. Bringing perpetrators of crimes to justice is the better act of love than allowing ourselves to be mistreated, and allowing the transgressors to go unpunished.

We may ask what the difference may be between bearing all things and enduring all things. It can be a little confusing, as even in the above verse 1Corinthians 9:12, the Greek word στέγομεν (*stegomen* (*we bear*)), is translated as *we endure*. And to make things even foggier, another aspect of love that we will cover in our current study verse of 1 Corinthians 13:7 is that love endures (the Greek word being ὑπομένει (*hupomenei))* all things.

So what is the difference between bearing and enduring? Perhaps a construction metaphor and the Greek etymology will help us out here. If bearing all things is related to the roof of a structure, then enduring all things is perhaps best related to the walls of the structure. The possible definitions of *hupomenei* are *to stand firm, to stay, to remain firm,* and *to wait*. Another way to look at enduring is that it represents a courageous resistance to hostile attacks.

The two terms are similar, just as a roof and the walls of a structure do similar things, and yet there are distinctions. Both offer protection and both withstand hostile forces. The way they provide stability is slightly different. The walls represent the more enduring stability of the structure and even hold the roof in place. However, the roof actually handles the brunt of the bad weather. It helps to withstand, divert and distribute the effects of the wind, lightning, rain, hail, sleet, snow and falling trees. The roof needs the walls, but the walls need the protection of the roof to be able to continue to stand firm. As we silently bear all things in love it prevents us from being known as a complainer, or worse, as a gossip.

Let us now look at the following additional scriptures:

God's View of Bearing all Things	
Galatians 6:2 *Bear one another's burdens, and thereby fulfill the law of Christ.*	Psalm 68:19 *Blessed be the Lord, who daily bears our burden, The God who is our salvation. Selah.*
Romans 15:1 *Now we who are strong ought to bear the weaknesses of those without strength and not just please ourselves.*	

Examples of Bearing all Things	
Psalm 89:50 *Remember, O Lord, the reproach of Your servants; How I bear in my bosom the reproach of all the many peoples,*	Jeremiah 10:19 *Woe is me, because of my injury! My wound is incurable. But I said, "Truly this is a sickness, And I must bear it."*
Mark 15:21–22 *They pressed into service a passer-by coming from the country, Simon of Cyrene (the father of Alexander and Rufus), to bear His cross.*	Exodus 18:22 *Let them judge the people at all times; and let it be that every major dispute they will bring to you, but every minor dispute they themselves will judge. So it will be easier for you, and they will bear the burden with you.*

Examples of Not Bearing all Things	
Genesis 4:13 *Cain said to the Lord, "My punishment is too great to bear!*	Luke 11:46 *But He said, "Woe to you lawyers as well! For you weigh men down with burdens hard to bear, while you yourselves will not even touch the burdens with one of your fingers.*

Perhaps these final words will also inspire us to bear all things in love.

Quotes

I counted dollars while God counted crosses.
I counted gains while He counted losses!
I counted my worth by the things gained in store.
But He sized me up by the scars that I bore.
I coveted honors and sought for degrees;
He wept as He counted the hours on my knees.
And I never knew 'til one day at a grave,
How vain are these things that we spend life to save! —*Selected*

There are no crownwearers in Heaven that were not crossbearers here below. —*Spurgeon*

When the late Bishop of Madras was visiting Travancore, there was introduced to him a little slave girl called "The Child Apostle." She had won this title by the zeal with which she talked of Christ to others. Her quiet, steady persistence in this had won several converts to Christ. But she had suffered persecution too brutal to relate. When she was introduced to the Bishop, her face, neck and arms were disfigured and scarred by stripes and blows. As he looked at her, the good man's eyes filled, and he said, "My child, how could you bear this?"

She looked up at him in surprise and said, "Don't you like to suffer for Christ, sir?" —*Choice Gleanings*

Adoniram Judson, the renowned missionary to Burma, endured untold hardships trying to reach the lost for Christ. For 7 heartbreaking years he suffered hunger and privation. During this time he was thrown into Ava Prison, and for 17 months was subjected to almost incredible mistreatment. As a result, for the rest of his life he carried the ugly marks made by the chains and iron shackles which had cruelly bound him.

Undaunted, upon his release he asked for permission to enter another province where he might resume preaching the Gospel. The godless ruler indignantly denied his request, saying, "My people are not fools enough to listen to anything a missionary might SAY, but I fear they might be impressed by your SCARS and turn to your religion!" —Henry G. Bosch

John Wesley was riding along a road one day when it dawned on him that three whole days had passed in which he had suffered no persecution. Not a brick or an egg had been thrown at him for three days.

Alarmed, he stopped his horse, and exclaimed, "Can it be that I have sinned, and am backslidden?"

Slipping from his horse, Wesley went down on his knees and began interceding with God to show him where, if any, there had been a fault.

A rough fellow, on the other side of the hedge, hearing the prayer, looked across and recognized the preacher. "I'll fix that Methodist preacher," he said, picking up a brick and tossing it over at him. It missed its mark, and fell harmlessly beside John. Whereupon Wesley leaped to his feet joyfully exclaiming, "Thank God, it's all right. I still have His presence." —J. G. Morrison

A young man was trying to establish himself as a peach grower. He had worked hard and invested his all in a peach orchard which blossomed wonderfully—then came a frost. He did not go to church the next Sunday, nor the next, nor the next. His minister went to see him to find the reason. The young fellow exclaimed: "I'm not coming any more. Do you think I can worship a God who cares for me so little that He will let a frost kill all my peaches?"

The old minister looked at him a few moments in silence, then said kindly: "God loves you better than He does your peaches. He knows that while peaches do better without frosts, it is impossible to grow the best men without frosts. His object is to grow men, not peaches." —Christian Worker's Magazine

XOgesis

Ned: “KJ, looks like you are building card houses to house dinosaurs?”

KJ: “The dinosaurs are monsters knocking the cavemen houses over.”

Ned: “How come some of the cards are so bent?”

KJ: “Well, uh, heh, heh, I guess my friend sort of got mad and he started to bend and rip the cards.”

Ned: “What did you do?”

KJ: “He started it by saying his card houses were stronger than mine. And when I threw a stegosaurus and knocked his over, I told him that if they were really strong even a stegosaurus couldn’t knock them over.”

KJ: “Then he turned into some kind of animal and started to step on my cards, and chew them and rip them. It was pretty gross how he acted. I would never do that.”

Ned: “Hmmm, don’t you think you could have just let that first comment slide. You know, just grin and bear it? You know, if you acted like a stegosaurus you could have avoided that argument.”

KJ: “Huh?”

Ned: “Did you know that stegosaurus actually means *roof lizard* or *covered lizard* from the Greek word, *stego*. And when the Bible says love *bear all things*, the Greek word for *bear* is *stego*. So if you would have acted like a stegosaurus instead of throwing a stegosaurus your friend would probably still be here playing with you.”

KJ: “I don’t know. If I acted like a stegosaurus my friend would probably have turned into a T-rex and eaten me and the cards.”

OLD TESTAMENT EXAMPLES [1Samuel 26] [The Book of Exodus]

Describe how the LORD ***Bears all Things*** or prevents us from not ***Bearing all Things*** in these passages.

Describe how the LORD has been ***Bearing with*** you and/or with someone that you know.

List a way you will ***Bear all Things*** this week. Prepare a concise teaching on ***Bearing all Things.***

My Application:

My Lesson Plan

Extra Credit – Pick any of the 10 commandments and think about how ***Bearing all Things*** will help you fulfill the commandment.

CHARACTERISTIC OF LOVE

Believes

Discussion

The word used in the Greek here for *believes*, πιστεύει (*pisteuei),* basically means *to trust or believe*. The noun form also has the meaning of *faith*. However, the use of the word *faith* in the context of 1 Corinthians 13 in verses two and thirteen makes it clear that the word used here in verse seven (*believes*) denotes more of a trust or confidence in people. While our own personal faith can move mountains, and though faith is one of the *big three* character qualities to seek after (faith, hope and love being the greatest), this use of belief/faith is not about what we have but how we think of others and what we instill in them.

Believing in another person does not mean that we will be naïve or gullible. We are not advocating what Proverbs warns us against.

Proverbs 14:15 *The naive believes everything, But the sensible man considers his steps.*

We can be fully aware of someone's past track record, but we also want to share in the person's future track record. We want to elevate people to higher levels, not remind them of where they are or have been. We can believe well of others before they are fully trustworthy or one hundred percent reliable. The fact that we may not have seen this person exhibit faithfulness is no reason for believing that the person is incapable of it.

Most people want to do a good job and be thought of as a person that can be trusted. People fail, sometimes miserably. People sometimes lose heart. People sometimes wonder themselves if they will be able to go on and turn failure into success. People wonder if they will be able to turn fear into courage. Amidst all of this uncertainty what really helps is a boost of trust, of belief, and of confidence. This is where we take our part in believing in others. We want to be used as an encouragement to people. We do not want to slip into skeptical, critical, fault-finding behavior that does nothing but decimate others. Elevate, do not decimate.

Now it is one thing to say that we believe in someone and another to give them some actual responsibility to prove our confidence in them. Sometimes it is a test of our faith to put faith in others and yet trust is one step beyond faith. Do we want to see people succeed? Trust in them. Do we want to see people move past the pain of failure? Trust in them. Do we want people to move past the numbness of fear? Trust in them. Do we want people to be at peace with God again? Give them a chance. Then give them another chance and another until the fire of the Holy Spirit is rekindled afresh in them. Simply put — believe in them.

Let us now look at the following additional scriptures:

God's View of Believing all Things	
John 21:15-17 *So when they had finished breakfast, Jesus said to Simon Peter, "Simon, son of John, do you love Me more than these?" He said to Him, "Yes, Lord; You know that I love You." He said to him, "Tend My lambs." He said to him again a second time, "Simon, son of John, do you love Me?" He said to Him, "Yes, Lord; You know that I love You." He said to him, "Shepherd My sheep." He said to him the third time, "Simon, son of John, do you love Me?" Peter was grieved because He said to him the third time, "Do you love Me?" And he said to Him, "Lord, You know all things; You know that I love You." Jesus said to him, "Tend My sheep."*	
Isaiah 35:3,4 *Encourage the exhausted, and strengthen the feeble. Say to those with anxious heart, Take courage, fear not. Behold, your God will come with vengeance; The recompense of God will come, But He will save you.*	Hebrews 3:13 *But encourage one another day after day, as long as it is still called "Today," so that none of you will be hardened by the deceitfulness of sin.*

Examples of Believing all Things	
Proverbs 31:11 *The heart of her husband trusts in her, And he will have no lack of gain.*	
1Samuel 23:16 *And Jonathan, Saul's son, arose and went to David at Horesh, and encouraged him in God.*	Acts 14:22 *strengthening the souls of the disciples, encouraging them to continue in the faith, and saying, "Through many tribulations we must enter the kingdom of God."*

Examples of Not Believing all Things	
Ezekiel 13:22 *Because you disheartened the righteous with falsehood when I did not cause him grief, but have encouraged the wicked not to turn from his wicked way and preserve his life,*	Acts 15:38 *But Paul kept insisting that they should not take him along who had deserted them in Pamphylia and had not gone with them to the work.*
1Kings 13:11 – 32 (an example of being gullible)	

Perhaps these final words will also inspire us to believe all things.

Quotes

As a boy, Marshall Rommel, later known as "the Desert Fox," was the laziest and most indolent student in his class. His teachers said he would never amount to anything. One schoolteacher said, "If Rommel ever shows up with a dictation without mistake we'll hire a band and go off for a day in the country."

At this the boy promptly sat up and soon turned in a dictation without one single error, showing that he could do it if there was sufficient inducement to spur him to the effort. But when the promised award was not forthcoming he promptly fell back into his old, indolent ways. But later on, fired by ambition to rise above the ranks, he became a bundle of driving energy and one of the ablest military men in the world. —Evangelistic Illustration

Courage is not the absence of fear; it is the mastery of it.

Oh, do not pray for easy lives. Pray to be stronger men. Do not pray for tasks equal to your powers. Pray for powers equal to your tasks.

It is a fine thing to have ability, but the ability to discover ability in others is the true test. —Elbert Hubbard

A good leader inspires other men with confidence in him; a great leader inspires them with confidence in themselves.

XOgesis

Ned: "Isn't fishing great! Hey, KJ, do you need help?"

KJ: "I can't figure this out!"

Ned: "Let me help you learn how to use your rod and reel to cast your lure."

KJ: "I can't do it, I am too afraid. What if I get it caught or hook myself or break the pole."

Ned: "I think you can do it. You just need practice to build your confidence."

KJ: "Why don't you just cast the line and then I'll hold it until a fish bites, then you reel the fish in?"

Ned: "But then you won't learn to be a confident fisherman."

KJ: "I'd rather have fish than confidence."

From KJ & Friends ™ © 2010 by G Doulos

OLD TESTAMENT EXAMPLES [Exodus 3-4:17] [1Kings 19]

Describe how the LORD ***Believes*** in us or displays His trust in us in these passages.

Describe how the LORD has been ***building up your confidence*** and/or someone that you know.

List a way you will ***Believe*** in someone this week. Prepare a concise teaching on ***Believing*** in others.

My Application:

My Lesson Plan

Extra Credit – Pick any of the 10 commandments and think about how ***Believing*** in others will help you fulfill the commandment.

CHARACTERISTIC OF LOVE

Discussion

The word used in the Greek here for *hopes,* ἐλπίζει *(elpizei),* basically means *to hope* or *to expect*. The implication is that which is hoped for is of a good and beneficial nature. Thus the idea behind this quality is that we would hope for the best in others and we would hope the best would happen to others. Most of the verses in the Bible use hope in reference to hoping in the Lord. By extension, we can say that the same favor and blessing we expect by hoping in the Lord, we can desire for others. Thus we hope for the Lord to bless them. Note that hoping in God is often translated as trusting in God or taking refuge in God.

When we hope for the best in others it leaves no room for unhealthy competition. Now we can spur others on by our example and our desire to do more for the Lord. We can do as the apostle Paul says, run the race to win. However, while we run the race to win, we also do not begrudge others that same victory. Even more than not begrudging people good things, hope will actually exhort others to achieve their (God-given) goals.

Hoping for the best for others is found in the family, in the workplace, in the church, and on the athletic field to name a few locations. When hope is not present it fosters sibling rivalry, a lack of sharing skills and information that could better people's careers, promotes internal church strife, and the unhealthy "i" in *win (*there is no "i" in *team).*

How do we adopt an attitude that promotes another's welfare (possibly literally a promotion, in the case of the workplace) as much or even above our own? One of the keys is to first recognize our own unique position and place in God's kingdom. While our goal may be to climb the ladder of dominance in terms of spiritual success, we should not be pushing people off the same ladder in order to get higher. Hoping in others is a top quality for disciple makers. We simply cannot make disciples if our goal is to make our selves look spiritually good and make others look spiritually not so good.

This can be subtle. Do we make derogatory comments (to others or just to ourselves) about those we do not like, respect or get along with? Do we secretly wish for or are just a little bit happy when we see the failure of some people? Or do we decide each day that we are going to help everyone we can get one step higher on the ladder? Or do we discuss among ourselves who is the greatest? That would not happen? What does Jesus say about this?

Mark 9:33-35 *They came to Capernaum; and when He was in the house, He began to question them, "What were you discussing on the way?" But they kept silent, for on the way they had discussed with one another which of them was the greatest. Sitting down, He called the twelve and said to them, "If anyone wants to be first, he shall be last of all and servant of all.*

So some of the keys to recognizing our own unique position and place in God's kingdom are to humble ourselves (before the Lord does), and to make it a priority to know Him, follow Him, deny ourselves and serve others. That will occupy so much of our time that we will not have much time left to worry about how high we are on the ladder compared to others. We have the right balance between being overly competitive and having a low self-esteem.

And in fact, if we are at the bottom of the ladder helping as many people get on as possible, is that not the highest position of all? Some of us may need to quit trying to be the first to get to the top and start helping people find that first and second rung on the ladder.

Hope will be the way. Hope will give us strength. Hope will keep our eyes on what is important. Hope is what we will instill in others. Hope is what will characterize our life.

Let us now look at the following additional scriptures:

God's View of Hoping all Things	
Jeremiah 29:11 *For I know the plans that I have for you, declares the Lord, plans for welfare and not for calamity to give you a future and a hope.*	
Psalm 31:24 *Be strong and let your heart take courage, All you who hope in the LORD.*	Psalm 32:10 *Many are the sorrows of the wicked, But he who trusts in the LORD, lovingkindness shall surround him.*

Examples of Hoping all Things	
1 Samuel 20 Jonathan, Saul's son encourages and protects David and recognizes him as the future king of Israel, despite the fact that he would be next in line to be king if Saul had his way.	John 3:30 *He must increase, but I must decrease.* – What John the Baptist said in relation to his ministry compared to the ministry of Jesus.
2 Kings 5:1-14 An Israelite slave girl captured by the Arameans when hearing of her mistress' husbands's (Naaman, captain of the army) leprosy, she still seeks his best by recommending that he go to see the prophet Elisha for healing.	Ruth Ruth, a Moabite, decides to stay with her mother-in-law, Naomi, an Israelite, after the death of both their husbands, and travel back to Israel in order to help and take care of Naomi.
Psalm 34:8 *O taste and see that the LORD is good; How blessed is the man who takes refuge in Him!*	Psalm 42:5 *Why are you in despair, O my soul? And why have you become disturbed within me? Hope in God, for I shall again praise Him For the help of His presence.*

Examples of Not Hoping all Things	
1 Kings 12:25-33 Jeroboam decides to create rival worship centers at Bethel and Dan because he fears losing his kingship (and his life) and would rather Israel not worship together at Jerusalem if it means he gets what he wants.	Mark 9:38-40 The disciple John and others when seeing a "rival" doing miracles told Jesus that they actually tried to stop him because he was not part of their group. Of course Jesus says no, as He states, "He who is not against us is for us..."
1 Samuel 18-5 - 27:4 Saul tries repeatedly to kill David because he fears that David will soon become king despite the fact that David has only helped him and served him well.	Genesis 4 The Lord has regard for Abel's offering and not Cain's. Instead of learning from Abel and admiring his ways, he decides to get rid of the competition.

Perhaps these final words will also inspire us to hope all things.

Quotes

A small boy was given two apples and told to divide them with his sister, and in doing so to be generous in giving her the larger one. He said finally, "Look Ma, you give her the apples and ask her to be generous."

In an old monastery near Bebenhausen, Germany, one may see two pairs of deer horns interlocked. They were found in that position many years ago. The deer had been fighting; their horns got jammed together and could not be separated; so they died. Dr. Kerr, who first told the story, added, "I would like to carry those horns into every house and school." We might add, "And into every church." —Harold P. Barker

XOgesis

KJ: "Great soccer game, Annie, but you should have crushed them even more. You were beating them three to nothing at half time. How come your coach switched everyone around?"

Annie: "She wants others to learn different positions and doesn't really care too much about the score. I'm glad she did 'cause I felt sorry for the other team."

KJ: "Felt sorry?! They are the enemy, they must be crushed or they will crush you."

Ned: "KJ has been playing too much World War III again. You know, there is a real world out there, where you can encourage and hope for good behavior instead of just shooting bad guys."

Annie: "Yeah, in your video game maybe you can talk to the bad guys and try and make friends with them instead of just shooting them."

KJ: "Well my goal is to make as many points as I can, and I don't score points by making friends."

Annie: "Maybe you should change your goals."

KJ: "Maybe your team should score more goals!!!"

Annie: "Hmmph, you are hopeless."

Ned: "Annie don't give up hope. KJ is still learning."

Annie: "Fine, you teach him."

OLD TESTAMENT EXAMPLES [1Kings 3:6-14] [Nehemiah 1:1-2:8]

Describe how the LORD shows that He is ***Hoping*** for the best for you, in these passages.

Describe how the LORD has been giving you ***Hope*** and/or someone that you know.

List a way you will ***Hope*** for the best for someone this week. Prepare a concise teaching on ***Hoping*** for the best in others.

My Application:

My Lesson Plan

Extra Credit – Pick any of the 10 commandments and think about how ***Hoping*** for the best in others will help you fulfill the commandment.

CHARACTERISTIC OF LOVE

Endures

Discussion

The word used in the Greek here for *endures*, ὑπομένει (*hupomenei*), has many senses such as: *stay behind, stay alive, stand firm, endure,* and *suffer*. This type of endurance is independent of reward or recognition and is instead motivated by love or honor or duty.

Nuances of this word include waiting for God with expectancy, and standing fast and persevering against worldly trials. And yet these two are one and the same, for how can we stand fast against Satan and his devices unless we await the direction and power of the Holy Spirit to provide our guidance, our deliverance and our victory.

Enduring is courage in the face of fire. Enduring is holding out until the bitter end. Enduring is staying in formation even when everything tells us to flee in fear. Enduring is cleaving to God. We cannot take up our cross daily unless we decide to endure all things. We can not consider it all joy when we fall into various trials unless we endure all things. We cannot rejoice when we are persecuted unless we resolutely decide to endure all things. We cannot put our hand to plow and never look back unless we endure all things.

If our motivation is not to be found in any personal rewards, then what will possess us to commit to such radical endurance of all that the world may throw our way to knock us down and out? What will keep us clinging to God as to a mast of a boat amidst a hurricane? What will enable us to endure all things? Let us review the following scriptures.

2 Timothy 2:10 *For this reason I endure all things for the sake of those who are chosen, so that they also may obtain the salvation which is in Christ Jesus and with it eternal glory.*

It is clear in this passage that Paul is enduring all things so that he may be used of God to spread the Gospel message. His desire for others to experience salvation is greater than any hardship he may face. Now that is dedication. His desire to see people make peace with God is what motivates him to endure.

Matthew 5:9 *Blessed are the peacemakers for they shall be called sons of God.*

Let us continue with some verses from the book of Hebrews.

Hebrews10:32-36 *But remember the former days, when, after being enlightened, you endured a great conflict of sufferings, partly by being made a public spectacle through reproaches and tribulations, and partly by becoming sharers with those who were so treated. For you showed sympathy to the prisoners and accepted joyfully the seizure of your property, knowing that you have for yourselves a better possession and a lasting one. Therefore, do not throw away your confidence, which has a great reward. For you have need of endurance, so that when you have done the will of God, you may receive what was promised.*

In this passage folks are reminded how they have endured persecutions for following Christ. These folks were also actively ministering and identifying with other fellow believers/prisoners who were being put to public spectacle. The desire to minister to others was more compelling than the accumulation of worldly possessions. We have good examples of this in Paul's fellow workers. Paul states in Philippians that he sent Timothy and Epaphroditus to them because they were genuinely concerned with their welfare. In fact, he states that Epaphroditus literally endured risking his life to minister to them. Timothy and Epahproditus viewed their own lives of little value compared to the value of others' lives. They were reliable, anything but lazy, *can-do* Christians!

Matthew 16:25 *For whoever wishes to save his life will lose it; but whoever loses his life for My sake will find it.*

And finally, we have one more good reason why we may be motivated to endure all things. Let us continue in Hebrews.

Hebrews 12:7 *It is for discipline that you endure; God deals with you as with sons; for what son is there whom his father does not discipline?*

While the reason we endure in the above passage is stated as *for discipline*, in reality, it is to please God. We allow God to shape our character through many things, both pleasant and painful. As we seek to stay within the will of God we have our rough edges sanded smooth. That friction can be tough to endure at times. Paul states in Philippians, chapter three, that he *suffered the loss of all things, and counted them but rubbish so that* he *may gain Christ.*

So what is the common thread throughout these three examples? Is the light bulb above our head shining?! The key to enduring all things is to be consumed with God and others. Are we beginning to understand what God meant for us to do when He gave us the two greatest commandments in the Old Testament? Jesus often repeated these as well. These commandments follow:

Deuteronomy 6:4,5 *"Hear, O Israel! The Lord is our God, the Lord is one! "You shall love the Lord your God with all your heart and with all your soul and with all your might.*

Leviticus 19:18 *You shall not take vengeance, nor bear any grudge against the sons of your people, but you shall love your neighbor as yourself; I am the Lord.*

Matthew 22:36-40 *"Teacher, which is the great commandment in the Law?" And He* [Jesus] *said to him, " 'You shall love the Lord your God with all your heart, and with all your soul, and with all your mind.' "This is the great and foremost commandment. "The second is like it, 'You shall love your neighbor as yourself.' "On these two commandments depend the whole Law and the Prophets."*

Let us now look at the following additional scriptures:

God's View of Enduring all Things	
James 1:12 *Blessed is a man who perseveres under trial; for once he has been approved, he will receive the crown of life which the Lord has promised to those who love Him.*	Isaiah 40:31 *Yet those who wait for the LORD Will gain new strength; They will mount up with wings like eagles, They will run and not get tired, They will walk and not become weary.*
Lamentations 3:25 *The Lord is good to those who wait for Him, To the person who seeks Him*	Job 22:21 *Yield now and be at peace with Him: Thereby good will come to you.*

Examples of Enduring all Things	
Hebrews 12:2 *fixing our eyes on Jesus, the author and perfecter of faith, who for the joy set before Him endured the cross, despising the shame, and has sat down at the right hand of the throne of God.*	1 Peter 2:20 *For what credit is there if, when you sin and are harshly treated, you endure it with patience? But if when you do what is right and suffer for it you patiently endure it, this finds favor with God.*
Job Noah	Jeremiah Daniel

Examples of Not Enduring all Things
Acts 15:38 *But Paul kept insisting that they should not take him* [Mark] *along who had deserted them in Pamphylia and had not gone with them to the work.*
1 Samuel 13:10-14 *As soon as he finished offering the burnt offering, behold, Samuel came; and Saul went out to meet him and to greet him. But Samuel said, "What have you done?" And Saul said, "Because I saw that the people were scattering from me, and that you did not come within the appointed days, and that the Philistines were assembling at Michmash, therefore I said, 'Now the Philistines will come down against me at Gilgal, and I have not asked the favor of the LORD.' So I forced myself and offered the burnt offering." Samuel said to Saul, "You have acted foolishly; you have not kept the commandment of the LORD your God, which He commanded you, for now the LORD would have established your kingdom over Israel forever. "But now your kingdom shall not endure. The LORD has sought out for Himself a man after His own heart, and the LORD has appointed him as ruler over His people, because you have not kept what the LORD commanded you."*

Examples of Not Enduring all Things
Jeremiah 38:17-19 *Then Jeremiah said to Zedekiah, "Thus says the* LORD *God of hosts, the God of Israel, 'If you will indeed go out to the officers of the king of Babylon, then you will live, this city will not be burned with fire, and you and your household will survive. 'But if you will not go out to the officers of the king of Babylon, then this city will be given over to the hand of the Chaldeans; and they will burn it with fire, and you yourself will not escape from their hand.' " Then King Zedekiah said to Jeremiah, "I dread the Jews who have gone over to the Chaldeans, for they may give me over into their hand and they will abuse me.*

Perhaps these final words will also inspire us to endure all things.

Quotes

The bee has been aptly described as "busy." To produce one pound of honey, the bee must visit 56,000 clover heads. Since each head has 60 flower tubes, a total of 3,360,000 visits are necessary to give us that pound of honey for the breakfast table. Meanwhile, that worker bee has flown the equivalent of three times around the world.

To produce one tablespoon of honey for our toast, the little bee makes 4,200 trips to flowers. He makes about ten trips a day to the fields, each trip lasting twenty minutes average and four hundred flowers. A worker bee will fly as far as eight miles if he cannot find a nectar flow that is nearer. Therefore, when you feel that persistence is a difficult task ... think of the bee.

William Wilberforce early became enflamed with the idea of stopping the slave trade and slavery in England. He succeeded in becoming a member of Parliament. Goaded by William Pitt, he spoke often against slavery and the slave trade but suffered repeated defeats in Parliament.

In 1807 he persuaded his colleagues to ban the slave trade. Not until 1833 did both houses of Parliament finally abolish slavery in Britain. The news of total victory came to Wilberforce on his deathbed. He was motivated in his life's career by an idea whose time finally came.

On a tablet in a church of Algiers is the name of "Devereux Spratt, 1641." The traveler inquires what that means, and he is told that Devereux Spratt, an Englishman, was captured with one hundred and twenty others in 1641 by the Algerian pirates. He was put to work with his fellow-slaves on the fortifications around Algiers. Cut off from congenial company, he looked to God for sympathy and strength, and God's grace proved, as always, sufficient.

Finding his fellow-captives full of despair, he began to cheer them with words of faith and hope; and soon he had gathered about him, through his faithful testimony, a little band of praying and worshipping Christians. Through the influence of his brother in England, after several years, Devereux Spratt was ransomed, and the order for his release was brought to the fortifications.

His fellow-captives rejoiced with tears at his good fortune, but expressed regret that their leader was to leave them. Devereux Spratt refused to accept the ransom, and remained until he died, a slave among slaves, that he might continue to comfort those whom God had brought to Christ through him.
—Current Anecdotes

When we give our final account to God, Let us only recount these ...

How much we counted on Him
How much others counted on us
What we counted as gain
What we counted as loss

— G Doulos

XOgesis

Naz: "So, looks like you've been to your church's trick-or-treatin' party. Are you supposed to be some type of a soldier?"

KJ: "I am a soldier for Christ, and now I know how tough it is."

Naz: "What do you mean?"

KJ: "I mean the whole time I was running around playing, and then having to lug tons of candy around, it was exhausting."

Naz: "Hmmm, well you look like a soldier, and talk like a soldier, but I doubt when the apostle Paul penned those words he had this in mind. Hey can I have one of those licorice candy things?"

KJ: "Back off."

Naz: "Whoa. Sorry. Geez!"

KJ: "A soldier always protects his prize."

Naz: "I thought you were a soldier for Christ."

KJ: "I am. I am pretending that the candy is the Gospel. So I must protect it."

Naz: "Actually shouldn't you be sharing this candy Gospel instead of protecting it?"

KJ: "Oh, OK. See what I mean? Being a soldier of Christ is tough. I do all the work and you get free candy."

Naz: "You are on to something!"

Old Testament Examples [1Peter 3:18-20] [Malachi 3&4]

Describe how the LORD ***Endures all things*** for us in these passages.

Describe how the LORD has been ***Enduring all things*** for you and/or someone that you know.

List a way you will ***Endure all things*** this week. Prepare a concise teaching on how to ***Endure all things***.

My Application:

My Lesson Plan

Extra Credit – Pick any of the 10 commandments and think about how ***Enduring all things*** will help you fulfill the commandment.

CHARACTERISTIC OF LOVE

Discussion

The word used in the Greek here for *fails*, πίπτει (*piptei*), basically means *to fall*. It can also be used to mean *to go under*, *to perish* and *to cease*. It is used to describe buildings that collapse due to earthquakes, the falling of crumbs from a table, the falling of stars from heaven, the literal falling of people (including being slain in battle) and animals. It can also be used in figurative senses as when a lot falls on someone, or when someone commits a sin, or falls away from following the truth.

In this verse the sense is akin to *not being defeated*, *not being brought to the ground*, and (using a double negative, not, not) *being able to stand*. Thus since love does *not fall* it does *not fail*. It should be noted that the Greek does not merely say that love *should* not fail, but in fact that love *never* fails. So we see a beautiful crescendo to our list of the characteristics of love. In all things or circumstances love bears, believes, hopes and endures, and in no circumstances will love ever fail. Thus we have reached the perfection in love that Jesus was talking about.

Matthew 5:43-48 *"You have heard that it was said, "You shall love your neighbor and hate your enemy." But I say to you, love your enemies and pray for those who persecute you, so that you may be sons of your Father who is in heaven; for He causes His sun to rise on the evil and the good, and sends rain on the righteous and the unrighteous. For if you love those who love you, what reward do you have? Do not even the tax collectors do the same? If you greet only your brothers, what more are you doing than others? Do not even the Gentiles do the same?" Therefore you are to be perfect, as your heavenly Father is perfect."*

Perhaps these final words will also inspire us to exhibit never failing love.

Quotes

I remember one precious experience with Henrietta Mears when we were having a sandwich in a hotel restaurant in St. Louis during a Christian bookseller's convention.

She began to reminisce about the wonderful things God had done in her life. She talked of the Lord Jesus as simply and genuinely as a new convert possessed by first love.

The tears flowed down her cheeks. It was thrilling to be with a Christian worker who had not become a pro. She really loved Jesus Christ, and she lived to make Him known. —Russell Hitt, Editor of Eternity

A little boy declared that he loved his mother "with all his strength." He was asked to explain what he meant by "with all his strength." He said: "Well, I'll tell you. You see, we live on the fourth floor of this tenement; and there's no elevator, and the coal is kept down in the basement. Mother is busy all the time, and she isn't very strong; so I see to it that the coal hold is never empty. I lug the coal up four flights of stairs all by myself. And it's a pretty big hold. It takes all my strength to get it up here...." —Gospel Herald

Dr. Alexander Maclaren used to tell of a man of great intellectual power whom he longed to win. To do so the famous preacher preached a whole series of sermons dealing with intellectual difficulties. To the doctor's delight, the man came shortly afterward and said he had become a convinced Christian and he wanted to join the church.

Overjoyed, the doctor said, "And which of my sermons was it that removed your doubts?" "Your sermons?" said the other. "It wasn't any of your sermons. The thing that set me thinking was that a poor woman came out of your church beside me and stumbled on the steps. When I put out my hand to help her, she smiled and said 'thank you' and then added, 'Do you love Jesus Christ my blessed Saviour? He means everything to me.' I did not then, but I thought about it. I found I was on the wrong road. I still have many intellectual difficulties, but now He means everything to me, too." —*Leslie D. Weatherhead*

A gentleman who was a professed Christian was taken seriously ill. He became troubled about the little love he felt in his heart for God, and spoke of his experience to a friend. This is how the friend answered him.

"When I go home from here, I expect to take my baby on my knee, look into her sweet eyes, listen to her charming prattle, and tired as I am, her presence will rest me; for I love that child with unutterable tenderness. But she loves me little. If my heart were breaking it would not disturb her sleep. If my body were racked with pain, it would not interrupt her play. If I were dead, she would forget me in a few days. Besides this, she had never brought me a penny, but was a constant expense to me. I am not rich, but there is not money enough in the world to buy my baby. How is it? Does she love me, or do I love her? Do I withhold my love until I know she loves me? Am I waiting for her to do something worthy of my love before extending it?"

This practical illustration of the love of God for His children caused the tears to roll down the sick man's face. "Oh, I see," he exclaimed, "it is not my love to God, but God's love for me, that I should be thinking of. And I do love Him now as I never loved Him before." —*Gospel Herald*

XOgesis

Teacher: "OK class let's see how you all did in using the letters of the word *love* as an acronym to describe what love means to you. Annie?"

Annie: "Leaving Others Very Encouraged."

Teacher: "Very nice! How about you KJ?"

KJ: "I have two. Like to Own Every Video game, and Laughing Obout ripping Video action Enemies!!"

Teacher: "Uh well, KJ, the acronym was only supposed to have the letters L-O-V-E and it was about love *itself*, not what *you* love."

Classmate Sid: "Yeah, ya goof. Besides Obout starts with an A. So your acronym would spell LARVAE which is a bunch of baby bugs. What a goofus."

KJ: "Well that makes sense because another thing I love to do is squash big *babies* who *bug* me like you, Sid."

Sid: "I can beat you in any video game."
KJ: "No, you can't."
Sid: "Yes, I can."
KJ: "No, you can't."

Teacher: "I had such good intentions..."

Sid: "Yes, I can."
KJ: "No, you can't."

OLD TESTAMENT EXAMPLES [You Find One !!!]

Describe how the LORD's ***Love Never Fails*** or prevents us from ***Failing,*** in these passages.

Describe how the LORD is showing His ***Never Failing Love*** for you and/or someone that you know.

List a way you will show ***Never Failing Love*** this week. Prepare a concise teaching on ***Love that Never Fails.***

My Application:

My Lesson Plan

Extra Credit – Review the table, *Love's Sweet Sixteen Summary* that follows. See if you can memorize all sixteen attributes of love (the first column).

Encore

Now that we have covered all of the characteristics of love we may be tempted to back-pedal a little and try and excuse ourselves from achieving the perfection that Jesus asks of us. We may say things like, *well, I am never going to be like that*, or *it is too hard for me to change,* or *I was born this way.*

Relatively recently, personality studies and leadership style studies have come into prominence. Based on research and how we answer certain questions we are categorized as a certain type of a personality, with the potential for exhibiting good and bad character qualities. Now while it is very obvious that two people can be completely different, for example, one can be quite extroverted (choleric and sanguine types) and the other quite introverted (melancholy and phlegmatic types), nevertheless the Lord would have all of us strive to imitate His example of perfect love.

As we look over the sixteen characteristics of love from our study, it may be intuitively obvious that some people with different personality traits may have an easier time mastering some of the aspects of love than others. Now in some senses that may be true, as those who have been given a special gifting from God may be a little more equipped to serve as a leader and as an example in that area. But the question needs to be asked: a leader or example for what purpose? One advantage of having spiritual leaders is that we have a living example that we can emulate. We may not all excel to the same degree in all sixteen characteristics of love, but we should be practicing all of them until they become perfected in our life. It is too easy to say, *well, I am just not going to get there,* or *it is too late for me.* Or we could say, *that other person is such a good example I do not need to be one.*

Wrong-o (old fashioned saying meaning *one is clearly mistaken*). There is a bumper sticker that says something like, *Jesus said it, I believe it, that settles it.* That needs to be our attitude as well with respect to treasuring our *First Love*, Jesus Christ, and reflecting that love in our lives.

The *measure of the pleasure in what we treasure* defines what is important to us. We must constantly be on guard to makes sure our treasure box is full of heavenly pursuits and not full of worldly items or pursuits. It is often the very pursuit of worldly items that limits the success in our spiritual pursuits. Jesus said we cannot serve God and mammon and so it is with love. Worldly pursuits will crowd out our love for God and our desire to serve Him.

1 John 2:15,16 *Do not love the world nor the things in the world. If anyone loves the world, the love of the Father is not in him. For all that is in the world, the lust of the flesh and the lust of the eyes and the boastful pride of life, is not from the Father, but is from the world.*

For young and old alike our first priority in life must always be our relationship with God, our *First Love*. Whether we are renewing or establishing a lifelong commitment; we are all seeking the same close relationship with God. God will never give up on us. His relationship with us is His first priority. And finally, as the Lord perfects His love in us, He will use us to perfect His love in others as well. So, do we want to change the world for Christ? We will, as Christ changes us into His definition of love. A key point of this study is that God's love for us empowers us to imitate that love to others.

The following table, *Love's Sweet Sixteen Summary,* summarizes the sixteen studies that we have gone through. We can come back to this well often to measure our progress and be amazed by all the many qualities of love that make our God so awesome! As a bonus, we have also included a table that compares our *sweet sixteen* to the nine *Fruit of the Spirit* and the *Ten Commandments.* Perhaps it can be improved upon. As an optional homework assignment, discuss other possible groupings for columns two and three. We have also summarized the positive teaching and corresponding negative admonitions into a paragraph in the form of a prayer. We can use the prayer each week to remind us of God's love for us and to review our path to becoming perfected in His love. Or even better (as another optional homework assignment), we can write out our very own prayer based on this study — dedicated to our *First Love! He would love it!*

Love's Sweet Sixteen Summary

NASB Wording	Alternate Word or Phrase	Without this quality we may become...
Is patient	Slow to anger	Insensitive, angry, unreasonable
Is kind	Beneficent, sympathetic	Stingy, unsympathetic
Is not jealous	Content, zealous for others	Envious, angry others have what we want or fearful they will take what we have, distrustful
Does not brag	Boasts on others, builds up others	Show-offs, tempting others to be jealous of us
Is not arrogant	Humble	Prideful, focused on our way of doing things, exaggerating our importance and self worth
Does not act unbecomingly	Decent	Rude, crude and lewd, socially insensitive and offensive
Does not seek its own	Selfless, a willing helper	Self absorbed, consumed with own problems
Is not provoked	Self-controlled	Overly sensitive, easily irritated
Does not take into account a wrong suffered	Seeks reconciliation	Bitter, someone who holds grudges, not truly forgiving
Does not rejoice in unrighteousness	Pure in heart	Double-minded, moral compromiser
Rejoices with the truth	Integrity	Dishonorable, corruptible, cowardly
Bears	Protects	A complainer, a gossip
Believes	Encourages	Skeptic, constant critic, fault-finder
Hopes	Exhorts	Overly competitive, low self-esteem
Endures	Suffers willingly, resolute	Not reliable, lazy, can't do attitude
Never fails	Perfect	Complacent

Love's Sweet Sixteen Compared

NASB Wording	Fruit of the Spirit	Ten Commandments
Is patient	Patience	Do not murder
Is kind	Kindness	Honor father and mother
Is not jealous	Gentleness	Do not covet
Does not brag	Gentleness	Do not covet
Is not arrogant	Gentleness	Honor father and mother
Does not act unbecomingly	Self-control	Do not commit adultery
Does not seek its own	Self-control	Do not steal
Is not provoked	Self-control	Do not murder
Does not take into account a wrong suffered	Peace	Do not murder
Does not rejoice in unrighteousness	Goodness	Do not bear false testimony
Rejoices with the truth	Joy	Remember the Sabbath
Bears	Faithfulness	Do not take God's name in vain
Believes	Faithfulness	Do not take God's name in vain
Hopes	Faithfulness	No idols
Endures	Faithfulness	No idols
Never fails	Love	No other Gods

Love. What I Want to Become.

I, Love, am patient and slow to anger. I am sensitive and willing to work with others without becoming overbearing or unreasonable. **I am kind**, beneficent, and sympathize with the plight of others and always generous. **I am never jealous**, envious or automatically mistrustful of anybody. I am extremely content with my life so far and yet zealous for others. **I never brag**, but rather build up and boast on others. I refrain from showing off because I do not want others to ever be jealous of my abilities. **I avoid arrogant** thoughts that exaggerate my own importance, while I live humbly and remind myself that I can always learn from others. **I do not act unbecomingly** but seek to be thought of as a decent human being. I avoid rude and crude talk and behavior and do not even joke about things that are socially insensitive. **I do not only seek my own** desires and needs. I am always willing to help others and not totally absorbed in solving my problems. I am selfless. **I am not easily provoked** but self-controlled so that I am not overly sensitive and do not get irritated at the drop of a hat. There is no chip on my shoulder. **I do not take into account a wrong suffered**. In fact, I try to forget the wrongs that people do because I seek reconciliation. I do not want to become a bitter, unforgiving person who holds grudges. However, **I never rejoice in unrighteousness** or view with pleasure things that go against God's Word. I do not compromise God's morals for anything and desire to be pure from the inside out. **I do rejoice in truth** found in God's Word. I am not afraid to associate myself with Christ and live out His Word in my life. I am integrity and honor, and will never corrupt His Holy Word. I am not a coward. **I bear** gladly hardships and other things so I can protect and serve. I do all of this quietly without complaint and would never think to complain about others behind their back. In fact, **I** am a great **believe**r in people and will always seek to encourage them every chance I get. I avoid being a skeptic, a critic and a fault-finder. **I** have great **hopes** for people and I exhort them to achieve their goals every chance I get. I have a positive self-image and am goal-oriented. However, I am not competitive to a point where I am glad others fail. **I endure** and suffer willingly all circumstances — for Christ's love compels me. I am resolute because it is Christ who strengthens me. I will never be thought of as an unreliable, lazy person who is always trying to get out of doing things. I am not only a *can-do* person but a *will-do* person. With all my heart, with all my soul, with all my mind, and with all my strength **I will** strive to **never fail** my Lord, my *First Love*. And, finally, I will never quit until Christ's love is perfected in me.

Bibliography

Aland, K., Black, M., Martini, C. M., Metzger, B. M., Robinson, M., & Wikgren, A. (1993; 2006). *The Greek New Testament, Fourth Revised Edition (Interlinear with Morphology)*. Deutsche Bibelgesellschaft.

Biblia Hebraica Stuttgartensia : With Westminster Hebrew Morphology. 1996 (electronic ed.). Stuttgart; Glenside PA: German Bible Society; Westminster Seminary.

Biblical Studies Press. (2006; 2006). *The NET Bible First Edition; Bible. English. NET Bible.; The NET Bible*. Biblical Studies Press.

Brenton, L. C. L. (1844). *The Septuagint Version of the Old Testament Translated into English*. London: Samuel Bagster and Sons.

Brown, F., Driver, S. R., & Briggs, C. A. (2000). *Enhanced Brown-Driver-Briggs Hebrew and English Lexicon* (electronic ed.). Oak Harbor, WA: Logos Research Systems.

Canne, J., Browne, Blayney, B., Scott, T., & Torrey, R. (2009). *The Treasury of Scripture Knowledge*. Bellingham, WA: Logos Research Systems, Inc.

Harris, R. L., Harris, R. L., Archer, G. L., & Waltke, B. K. (1999). *Theological Wordbook of the Old Testament* (electronic ed.). Chicago: Moody Press.

Kittel, G., Friedrich, G., & Bromiley, G. W. (1995). *Theological Dictionary of the New Testament*. Grand Rapids, MI: W.B. Eerdmans.

Liddell, H. (1996). *A Lexicon : Abridged from Liddell and Scott's Greek-English Lexicon*. Oak Harbor, WA: Logos Research Systems, Inc.

Louw, J. P., & Nida, E. A. (1996). *Greek-English Lexicon of the New Testament : Based on Semantic Domains* (electronic ed. of the 2nd edition.). New York: United Bible societies.

Merriam-Webster, I. (1996). *Merriam-Webster's Collegiate Dictionary*. (10th ed.). Springfield, Mass., U.S.A.: Merriam-Webster.

New American Standard Bible : 1995 update. 1995. LaHabra, CA: The Lockman Foundation.

Robertson, A. (1997). *Word Pictures in the New Testament.* Oak Harbor: Logos Research Systems.

Strong, J. (1996). *Enhanced Strong's Lexicon* (electronic ed.). Ontario: Woodside Bible Fellowship.

Strong, J., S.T.D., LL.D. (2009). *A Concise Dictionary of the Words in the Greek Testament and The Hebrew Bible.* Bellingham, WA: Logos Research Systems, Inc.

Swanson, J. (1997). *Dictionary of Biblical Languages with Semantic Domains : Greek (New Testament)* (electronic ed.). Oak Harbor: Logos Research Systems, Inc.

Swete, H. B., D.D. (2009). *The Old Testament in Greek: According to the Septuagint (Text).* Bellingham, WA: Logos Research Systems, Inc.

Tan, P. L. (1996, c1979). *Encyclopedia of 7700 Illustrations* : A treasury of illustrations, anecdotes, facts and quotations for pastors, teachers and Christian workers. Garland TX: Bible Communications.

Tan, R., deSilva, D. A., & Logos Research Systems, I. (2009; 2009). *The Lexham Greek-English Interlinear Septuagint.* Logos Research Systems, Inc.

The Holy Bible: King James Version. 2009 (Electronic Edition of the 1900 Authorized Version.). Bellingham, WA: Logos Research Systems, Inc.

The Holy Bible: New International Version. 1996 (electronic ed.). Grand Rapids, MI: Zondervan.

Theological Dictionary of the New Testament. 1964- (G. Kittel, G. W. Bromiley & G. Friedrich, Ed.) (electronic ed.). Grand Rapids, MI: Eerdmans.

The Revised Standard Version. 1971. Oak Harbor, WA: Logos Research Systems, Inc.

Thomas, R. L. (1998). *New American Standard Hebrew-Aramaic and Greek Dictionaries : Updated Edition.* Anaheim: Foundation Publications, Inc.

Vincent, M. R. (2002). *Word Studies in the New Testament.* Bellingham, WA: Logos Research Systems, Inc.

Walvoord, J. F., Zuck, R. B., & Dallas Theological Seminary. (1983-). *The Bible Knowledge Commentary: An Exposition of the Scriptures*. Wheaton, IL: Victor Books.

Wiersbe, W. W. (1996). *The Bible Exposition Commentary*. Wheaton, Ill.: Victor Books.

Wuest, K. S. (1997). *Wuest's Word Studies from the Greek New Testament : For the English Reader*. Grand Rapids: Eerdmans.

How Many Bytes in Human Memory? by Ralph C. Merkle
This article first appeared in Foresight Update No. 4, October 1988.

www.ingramcontent.com/pod-product-compliance
Lightning Source LLC
Chambersburg PA
CBHW081513040426
42447CB00013B/3207

* 9 7 8 0 6 1 5 4 4 5 1 1 3 *